"In 1983, Randy Miller combined his extens[ive knowledge of New England] fiddle music with his organizational and cal[ling skills to produce The New] England Fiddler's Repertoire, a tune book ge[m that not only provided contra (and other) musicians with a core repertoire but also served as an inspiration for the tune books that followed. The timelessness of the music and the elegance and accessibility of the notation in NEFR insure that it will be an invaluable resource for years to come. Thank you, Randy!"

— Sue Songer, Portland, OR. Contra dance pianist and fiddler, founder of the Portland Megaband with 75 dance musicians, and co-publisher of *The Portland Collection* (1 and 2).

"The *New England Fiddler's Repertoire* is one of the few tune books that I recommend without reservation. It's a great source of classic versions of New England contra dance tunes. These tunes, with Celtic and French Canadian roots, are the bedrock of traditional New England fiddling."

— Jay Ungar, Saugerties, NY. Fiddler, composer, and co-host with Molly Mason of Ashokan Fiddle & Dance Camps.

"NEFR was one of the first tune books in my collection and I'm really excited about the newest edition. There is a lot of nostalgia among young folk fiddlers about learning tunes by ear; and it's true, you really gotta listen! But seriously, have you ever played that game where you all sit in a circle and whisper something in your neighbor's ear—you go around the circle until the phrase comes back pretty different from the original? Yeah...this is why we write things down. If we are truly honest with ourselves about preserving traditional dance tunes, solid references like NEFR are indispensable. This tune book captures a taste of New England and preserves it for eternity."

— Michael Ludgate, Ithaca, NY. Dancer, musician, and host of a beginner-friendly contra tune jam.

"I'm excited to hear about the 25th anniversary edition of *New England Fiddler's Repertoire* and can't wait to add it to my collection. I still have my well-worn 1983 edition, but I also value the 2003 edition with its chord suggestions and lovely Randy Miller woodcuts. Thanks for keeping all those great old tunes alive and well!!"

— Bob Dalsemer, Coordinator of the Music and Dance Programs, John C. Campbell Folk School, Brasstown, NC.

"Randy Miller has been a fixture in New England fiddling for more than 30 years, and his deep knowledge of the genre shows in this collection. The *New England Fiddler's Repertoire* is an important document of the music traditionally played for contradancing in New England. These are the tunes everyone needs to know!"

— Donna Hébert, Amherst, MA. Fiddler, master teacher, and member of Groovemama and the Franco-American heritage band, Chanterelle.

"NEFR is an essential source for any musician starting to play for contra dances, and an inexhaustible, ever useful source of tunes for existing bands. All the old standard tunes are there, complete with guitar/piano chords. A must for any serious dance musician!"
—Ralph Sweet, Hazardville, CT. Square and contradance caller since 1948, maker of wooden flutes, whistles and fifes.

"In my travels, I've learned that I will invariably give away my latest copy of *New England Fiddler's Repertoire* to someone who asks 'What's the one best source for those old time dance tunes?' From Alaska to Alabama to Denmark, I've sat in on sessions where NEFR was the definitive source for the music dancers love. Among musicians in one Midwestern city, it's even referred to as 'the bible'. You hold in your hands the latest, most annotated, and easiest-to-use edition of this classic. Now get busy and practice!"
—Mary DesRosiers, Harrisville, NH. Dance caller, musician, folklorist, and performer of New England singing games.

"NEFR is an invaluable resource, and should be in the fiddle case of every literate dance fiddler in the Northeast."
—Greg Boardman, Lewiston, ME. Fiddler, string teacher, and founder of the Maine Fiddle Camp.

"Most of the time Jacqueline and I work the gigs alone. We do not utilize the dots. We have scraps of paper with notation on them, but never can find them. HOWEVER, we do carry NEFR with us. We always welcome sit-ins, many of whom require the dots, so NEFR comes in handy. The other day we were playing on an island off the coast of NH, and hadn't lugged our stuff out there. Just the fiddles. Chap asks to sit in. Uses the little fellers on the page. We needed Cock of the North. By god he's got a copy of NEFR. The day is saved."
—Dudley Laufman, Canterbury, NH. Dance musician and caller since 1948, poet, and with Jacqueline Laufman forms the band, Two Fiddles.

"I love the New England Fiddler's Rep book and always take it with me on the road. It has provided me with a firm foundation in traditional New England fiddle tunes, from sweet, pretty, simple music to real finger-twisters. Fantastic collection, and a great book for every fiddler!"
—Eden MacAdam-Somer, fiddle performer in traditional, jazz, bluegrass, western swing, and classical, member of the Boston-based band Notorious.

"This book is the contra dance music gold standard, the benchmark against which all other collections are measured. The author's experience, industry and unflinching good taste create a true 'must have'. Get some copies now and give most of them to your best friends."
—Warren Argo, Olympia, WA. Musician, caller, dancer, sound-system operator, and festival organizer.

New England Fiddler's Repertoire

A Source Book of Established Contra Dance Music
Compiled by Randy Miller and Jack Perron,
with an Introduction by Newton F. Tolman

Third Edition
25th Anniversary, 1983-2008
Edited by Robert Bley-Vroman and Randy Miller

Revised, with Tunes Arranged Alphabetically by Title,
Chords Added, and a List of Tunes by Key

Illustrated by Fran Tolman (cover) and Randy Miller

FIDDLECASE BOOKS®

New England Fiddler's Repertoire
First printing 1983
Second printing 1986
Third printing 1990
Fourth printing 1992
Fifth printing 1996
Sixth printing 2000
2nd Edition: First printing 2003
2nd Edition: Second printing 2004
3rd Edition: First printing 2007

Third Edition Copyright © 2007 by Randy Miller
Second Edition Copyright © 2003 by Randy Miller
First Edition Copyright © 1983 by Randy Miller and Jack Perron

All rights reserved. Printed in the United States of America

ISBN–13: 978-0-9770530-6-3
ISBN–10: 0-9770530-6-7

The second edition of this book was produced with assistance from the Gadd/Merrill Fund of the Country Dance and Song Society.

The wood engraving by Randy Miller on page 15 is of a contra dance in the Nelson town hall. It originally appeared in A Time to Dance: American Country Dancing from Hornpipes to Hot Hash by Richard Nevell (St. Martin's Press, 1977), and is used by permission.

Other Fiddlecase Books® publications:
The Fiddler's Throne
The Fiddler's Throne – CD
Irish Traditional Fiddle Music
William Marshall's Scottish Melodies
The Fiddler's Friend

Published and distributed by Randy Miller, 17 North Road, Alstead, NH 03602

International ordering online at www.randymillerprints.com

CONTENTS

About the Third Edition..vi

Notes to the Second Edition..................................vi

How the Second Edition Came To Be..................vii

Introduction..viii

Foreword...x

Dedication...xi

Alphabetical List of Tunes...................................xii

List of Tunes by Key..xiv

List of Alternate Titles..xvi

Original Order of Tunes, 1983.........................xviii

Tunes..1-94

Blank staff *(see back of book)*

About the Third Edition

Happy 25th birthday, NEFR! In this age of communications wizardry, for a book (of traditional fiddle music, no less) to remain in print for 25 years is quite an acheivement. It is truly gratifying that the continued interest in the dance music of the Northeast—represented here by 168 classic tunes—has kept *New England Fiddler's Repertoire* in print for such a lengthy spell.

Added to this third edition, at the request of several musicians, is a list giving the original '83 order of tunes which had the jigs grouped together, separated out from the reels, marches, and hornpipes. The two subsequent editions have the tunes in alphabetical order, a more convenient arrangement. For this 3rd edition, the time signatures for several tunes have been corrected to give them an appearance more readily useful to the contra dance musician; also refinements to a few of the tune melodies as well as to the back-up chord progressions have been made in an attempt to improve the music. In this, the editors were guided by the maxim, "less is more."

I would like to thank all of the musicians, too numerous to name, who have given me feedback, encouragement, and their stamp of approval after the appearance of edition 2. For edition 3, special thanks are due to Deb Keller and Eric Anderson for their kind support.

—RM

Notes to the Second Edition

About a year ago I received an email from a friend, contra piano-player and caller Robert Bley-Vroman. It was filled with suggestions and ideas on how to improve one of his favorite tune books. "I think it would be doing a big favor to traditional dance music to put out a new edition of the *Repertoire*," he wrote. His enthusiasm was infectious and we decided to collaborate on a revised, second edition of NEFR.

So what's new? The music is easier to read, an improvement over the hand-written notation used in the 1983 edition. And chords to help accompanists have been added to the music. Just as the tunes themselves are established traditional settings, in a sense "musical antiques," so the chords offered here reflect an overall sound that cannot be confused with any other American musical genre or style. Although we do not advocate a slavish adherence to melody line or chord progression, and indeed take pleasure in playing and listening to variations, nevertheless these tunes are musical inheritances. Whatever the fiddler's bowing, accent, or melody-line variation (and likewise the accompanist's choice of chording and rhythm), judicious use of these will help preserve the unique flavor of New England fiddle music.

Also new to the second edition is an alphabetical list of tunes, a key index by meter, a list of alternate titles, and a sturdier book binding to hold everything together. The added illustrations inside the book are my own wood engravings, that is, prints made from hand-engraved boxwood blocks.

Has it really been twenty years since NEFR first came out? It seems like a span of about what it takes to fiddle "Chorus Jig" seven or eight times on some town hall stage, while watching the contra dancers clatter up and down the floor! And just as a fiddler improves by playing something over and over, I hope this new edition (and seventh overall printing) of NEFR provides an ever better source for contra dance musicians.

—Randy Miller
E. Alstead, N.H.
March, 2003

How the Second Edition Came To Be

A few years ago, our rhythm pianist extraordinaire, Jim Fownes, left Hawai'i for Massachusetts. I had been calling dances in Honolulu for some years, and now, faced with a piano-less band, I decided to try my hand at playing. But, how to practice most efficiently? Of course I had the *New England Fiddler's Repertoire*, which contains all the old tunes I have always loved best to dance to. At about the same time, revolutionary developments were taking place in computer music notation and playback. Chris Walshaw had invented abc notation in 1991, and tools were becoming available to play this notation on personal computers. Why not transcribe the *Repertoire* in abc? I did so, and with my old Powerbook on top of the grand, I beat away to my heart's content, with a melody player of infinite patience at my disposal. (Once, after three hours of pounding, the neighbors came over to complain.) I fooled around with chords and wrote down the ones that sounded good. As I played, I became increasingly impressed by the inherent danceability of this music.

Since the original publication of the *Repertoire*, there has been an explosion in contra dance music. Musicians have moved well beyond the core of tunes that long supported New England dance. New sources of traditional music have been tapped and great new tunes composed. I discovered, as I traveled around the country playing for dances and at jam sessions, that musicians who are newly come to contra dance are sometimes unacquainted with the long-established tunes. They may not know "Lady Walpole's Reel" or "Rory O'More."

Randy Miller and I decided the time was right for a new publication of the *Repertoire*, newly edited and typeset, with chords. These are the tunes that have made dances come alive, for centuries. We hope this collection will play an important part in the revival that this music deserves.

This edition was transcribed in abc with the aid of Phil Taylor's Barfly for the Macintosh. Typesetting was done using Michael Methfessel's abc2ps.

—Robert Bley-Vroman
Honolulu, Hawai'i
June, 2003

Introduction

Last year a man with an English accent phoned from Boston, wanted to come up next afternoon to consult me about playing contra dance music. It was his first trip to the U.S., but he arrived here in good order in a rented car shortly after lunch, armed with a tape recorder, some tapes, music stand, fiddle case, and a copy of our *Nelson Music Collection,* which someone had given him. He was first violinist in a leading British symphony orchestra on tour, it turned out, and he had fallen madly in love with our tunes, many of them very difficult contras. It was something new to him, and he wondered where they came from. Of course he didn't know that all these tunes had come to us, long ago, from Britain. At least, all the older ones.

Contra dance tunes to us, for at least a century, have been whatever kind of tune the dancers liked best. There were no ethnic boundaries. So long as the tempo was quick enough and the rhythm well suited, our tunes ranged from French Canadian to British Isles to ancient Macedonian Greek.

We have in our tiny, remote village of Nelson, New Hampshire, an old town hall, long a shrine to the square dance faithful, cradle of callers like Ralph Page and Dudley Laufman and famous musicians like Quig (Albert Quigley), myself, Cousin Harve (Harvey Tolman), and a hundred others. Nelson contra dances stayed in business for half a century when they were virtually unknown elsewhere. Perhaps because the dancers, the callers, the musicians did it purely for love of the thing, had other major occupations, and weren't relying on their music-dance efforts for profits. We were out to have a good time.

Someone once asked, who was Nelson's best square-dancer? Well, in the last 75 years according to old experts I remember hearing, it would have to be Walter Hall. He was a strapping fellow who stood about 6' 4". The Hall farm homestead was just beyond the present huge O.K. Fairbanks shopping plazas, going toward West Keene. Hard to believe now, but when I first knew Walter in 1922, there were just a few places, mostly farms, from the brick mills by the river, all the way out to the then small village of West Keene.

Walter is still around. Last year the *Keene Sentinel* had a feature about him, with photos of him running a maple-syrup evaporator up in Westmoreland. And I'm hoping he will come to a party I'm having next month. For years, Walter was famous for a brew less sweet but more rare—the fanciest champagne cider we ever tasted. (His mother used to tell us, "Walter is just like his late father—he's got a hollow leg!")

Hollow or not, Walter's legs almost stopped the dance, when the crowd saw him spin around with his partner, on one foot, the other raised higher than his head. But his masterpiece was swinging his partner aloft like a pinwheel, her feet flying around above the heads of the next couples in line...

Still single, in the '30s, Walter arrived one warm spring night at Intermission of the dance. As we all filed out of the hall to get some air or whatever, Walter was driving his big, long, classic old Packard convertible slowly around the village green. In the rumble seat was a large barrel and box of paper cups. Walter was yelling, "Come one, come all! We've broached the cider! Come one, come all!" He parked right at the front door of the hall, and started passing out the cider to "one and all." Nobody at *that* dance ever forgot Walter, or his cider.

By now it seems I'm writing ancient history; well, right, in Nelson dance annals.

I've enjoyed playing with Jack Perron and Randy Miller over several years at many rousing, rollicking occasions. I would say they have assembled a superb collection here.

—Newton F. Tolman
Greengate, Nelson, N.H.
March 20, 1983

Foreword

Musicians interested in the traditional contra dance music of New England have had access to a large number of published collections. However, the books available until now have either contained a vast number of eclectic tunes (Cole's *One Thousand Fiddle Tunes,* for example), or conversely, only a few highly selective ones such as are found in the *Nelson Music Collection*. It has been necessary to acquire several books in order to have access to an appropriate range of contra dance music.

The purpose of *New England Fiddler's Repertoire* is to make available in one book a standard collection of contra dance music. Included in these 168 tunes are old favorites as well as lesser-known yet classic fiddle tunes. Rather than a definitive volume, the book represents a modest source book of established tunes eminently suited to contra dancing. In compiling this collection the editors have drawn on twenty-six years' combined experience performing contra dance music while working with most of the New England callers.

This book does not include music specifically designated for squares or quadrilles, although some tunes may be naturally suitable, nor does it contain tunes of recent composition, as the intent has been to include well-established older tunes. Some newly composed tunes have indeed come into general use such as "Scotty O'Neil" (Bob McQuillen), "Glen Towle" (Dudley Laufman), and "McQuillen's Squeezebox" (Ralph Page) and are found in published collections of new music. Further, with but one exception—the "Gay Gordons"—the book does not include music for couple dances, and we leave this aspect of dancing to the particular preferences of the various callers and dance leaders.

The front cover illustration is a lino cut by Fran Tolman published in the original 1937 edition of *The Country Dance Book* by Beth Tolman and Ralph Page, and used here by kind permission of Mrs. Florence Tolman.

The dancing of contras has recently spread nation-wide from its New England roots, and by presenting this collection of contra dance music we hope to promote the enjoyment of dancing everywhere.

—Randy Miller
East Alstead, N.H.
March, 1983

Newton F. Tolman
1909—1986

Newt Tolman was born and raised on ancestral farmlands in Nelson, New Hampshire. Taught to play the flute at age nine by an uncle, he later made concert tours of New England, recorded several albums, and was a stalwart musician at the Nelson square dances for more than four decades.

A writer and composer, he published the *Nelson Music Collection,* an early reference book for contra dance musicians. He also wrote *Quick Tunes and Good Times,* a musical autobiography which includes a history of New England square and contra dance music with stories about local musicians.

He was characteristically enthusiastic and innovative with music. When not playing, he could be seen waving his instrument in the air to the beat of the music from his seat on the stage. At one Nelson dance he brought a rare bass flute to play. He was always supportive of younger musicians and encouraged the playing of traditional contra dance music. This book is affectionately dedicated to Newt Tolman.

ALPHABETICAL LIST OF TUNES
Tunes arranged by Randy Miller

All the Way to Galway
Allie Crocker's Reel
La Bastringue
Batchelder's Reel
Bell's Favorite
Belles of Tipperary
Big John McNeil
Blackberry Quadrille
Blackthorn Stick
Bonnie Dundee
Brisk Young Lads
Broken Lantern
Cattle in the Crops
Chatagee Reel
Chorus Jig
Cincinnati Hornpipe
Cock o' the North
Coleraine
Come Dance and Sing
Come Up the Back Stairs
Connaught Man's Rambles
Constitution Hornpipe
Corn Rigs
Crooked Stovepipe
Deerfoot
Democratic Rage Hornpipe
Devil's Dream
Durang's Hornpipe
Earl of Mansfield
Far from Home
Farewell to Whiskey
Finnegan's Wake
Fireman's Reel
Fisher's Hornpipe
Flowers of Edinburgh
Forester's Hornpipe
Les Fraises et les Framboises
Galopede
Gandy Dancer's Reel
Gaspé Reel
Gay Gordons

Glise à Sherbrooke
Green Fields of America
Green Mountain Petronella
La Grondeuse
Growling Old Man and Woman
Happy to Meet, Sorry to Part
Haste to the Wedding
High Level Hornpipe
Hull's Victory
Hullichan Jig
Hundred Pipers
Il est Né
Indian Reel
Inimitable Reel
Irish-American Reel
Irishman's Heart to the Ladies
Jackson's Fancy
Jacques Cartier
Jefferson and Liberty
Jenny's Gone to Linton
Reel des Jeunes Mariés
Jimmy Allen
Jock Tamson's Hornpipe
Joys of Wedlock
Judy's Reel
Kenmure's Up and Awa'
Kitty McGee
Lady on the Boat
Lady Walpole's Reel
Lamplighter's Hornpipe
Lanigan's Ball
Lardner's Reel
Larry O'Gaff
Levantine's Barrel
Lillibulero
Little Burnt Potato
Little Judique
Mackilmoyle
Maggie Brown's Favorite
Maguinnis' Delight
Mairi's Wedding

Maple Leaf Jig
Mason's Apron
Meeting of the Waters
Miller's Reel
Miss McCleod's Reel
Money Musk
Reel de Montréal
Morning Star
Morpeth Rant
Mother's Reel
Mountain Ranger
Muckin' o' Geordie's Byre
Munster Buttermilk
Munster Lass
My Love's But a Lassie
New Rigged Ship
O'Donnell Abu
Off She Goes
L'Oiseau Bleu
Old French
Opera Reel
Paddy on the Railroad
Paddy on the Turnpike
Paddy Whack
Pays de Haut
Peter Street
Petronella
Pigtown Fling
Piper's Lass
Poppy Leaf Hornpipe
Portland Fancy
President Garfield's Hornpipe
President Grant's Hornpipe
President Lincoln's Hornpipe
Prince William
Quindaro Hornpipe
Rakes of Clonmel
Rakes of Mallow
Red-Haired Boy
Red Lion
Rickett's Hornpipe
Road to Boston
Rock Valley

Roddy McCorley
Rolling Off a Log
Ronfleuse Gobeil
Rory O'More
Rose Tree
Ross's Reel #4
Saddle the Pony
Saint Anne's Reel
Saint Lawrence Jig
Saint Patrick's Day in the Morning
Scotch Hornpipe
Set de la Baie St. Paul
Shandon Bells
Sheehan's Reel
Ships are Sailing
Smash the Windows
Smith's Reel
Snowflake Hornpipe
Snowshoer's Reel
Snowy-Breasted Pearl
Soldier's Cloak
Speed the Plow
Spitfire Reel
Starr Label Reel
Starry Night for a Ramble
Staten Island Hornpipe
Steamboat Quickstep
Stool of Repentance
Swallowtail Jig
Swallowtail Reel
Swinging on a Gate
Teetotaler's Reel
The Tempest
Tenpenny Bit
Reel de Ti-Jean
'Tis the Gift to be Simple
Top of Cork Road
La Toque Bleue
Vinton's Hornpipe
Walker Street
White Cockade
Wind That Shakes the Barley
Woodchopper's Reel

LIST OF TUNES BY KEY

Reels, Hornpipes, Marches

Key of G
Chatagee Reel
Crooked Stovepipe
Far from Home
Farewell to Whiskey
Flowers of Edinburgh
Les Fraises et les Framboises
Galopede
Glise à Sherbrooke
Green Fields of America
Green Mountain Petronella
Il est Né
Indian Reel
Inimitable Reel
Jimmy Allen
Levantine's Barrel
Mairi's Wedding
Miss McCleod's Reel
Reel de Montréal
Morning Star
O'Donnell Abu
Pigtown Fling
Poppy Leaf Hornpipe
Quindaro Hornpipe
Rakes of Mallow
Sheehan's Reel
Swinging on a Gate
Teetotaler's Reel
'Tis the Gift to be Simple
La Toque Bleue
Walker Street
White Cockade

Key of D
All the Way to Galway
Allie Crocker's Reel
La Bastringue
Belles of Tipperary
Chorus Jig
Cincinnati Hornpipe
Come Dance and Sing
Corn Rigs
Durang's Hornpipe
Finnegan's Wake
Forester's Hornpipe
Gandy Dancer's Reel
Gaspé Reel
La Grondeuse
Jacques Cartier
Reel des Jeunes Mariés
Jock Tamson's Hornpipe
Judy's Reel
Little Judique
Mackilmoyle
Morpeth Rant
My Love's But a Lassie
L'Oiseau Bleu
Old French
Opera Reel
Paddy on the Railroad
Pays de Haut
Petronella
Piper's Lass
Rickett's Hornpipe
Road to Boston
Roddy McCorley
Ronfleuse Gobeil
Rose Tree
Scotch Hornpipe
Set de la Baie St. Paul
Smith's Reel
Saint Anne's Reel
Staten Island Hornpipe
Reel de Ti-Jean
Wind That Shakes the Barley
Woodchopper's Reel

Key of A
Big John McNeil
Devil's Dream
Earl of Mansfield
Fireman's Reel
Gay Gordons
Jenny's Gone to Linton
Lamplighter's Hornpipe
Lardner's Reel
Mason's Apron
Meeting of the Waters
Miller's Reel
Money Musk
Peter Street
Pres. Lincoln's Hornpipe
Prince William
Red-Haired Boy
Snowflake Hornpipe
Snowy-Breasted Pearl
Speed the Plow
Starr Label Reel

Key of C
Mother's Reel

Key of F
Batchelder's Reel
Constitution Hornpipe
Deerfoot
Fisher's Hornpipe
Hull's Victory
Irish-American Reel
Maguinnis' Delight
Ross's Reel #4
Snowshoer's Reel

Key of Bb
Democratic Rage Hornpipe
High Level Hornpipe
Lady Walpole's Reel
Mountain Ranger
Pres. Garfield's Hornpipe
Pres. Grant's Hornpipe
Red Lion
Spitfire Reel
Vinton's Hornpipe

Key of Am
Growling Old Man & Woman

Key of Em
Ships are Sailing
Swallowtail Reel

Key of Gm
Paddy on the Turnpike

Jigs

Key of G
Blackthorn Stick
Bonnie Dundee
Come Up the Back Stairs
Hullichan Jig
Joys of Wedlock
Larry O'Gaff
Maggie Brown's Favorite
Maple Leaf Jig
Munster Buttermilk
Saddle the Pony
St. Patrick's Day in the Morning
The Tempest

Key of D
Bell's Favorite
Blackberry Quadrille
Cattle in the Crops
Connaught Man's Rambles
Haste to the Wedding
Jackson's Fancy
Kitty McGee
Lady on the Boat
Little Burnt Potato
Muckin' o' Geordie's Byre
New Rigged Ship
Off She Goes
Shandon Bells
Saint Lawrence Jig
Smash the Windows
Starry Night for a Ramble
Soldier's Cloak
Top of Cork Road

Key of A
Cock o' the North
Hundred Pipers
Irishman's Heart to the Ladies
Kenmure's Up and Awa'
Lillibulero
Paddy Whack
Portland Fancy
Rory O'More
Steamboat Quickstep
Stool of Repentance

Key of C
Broken Lantern
Rock Valley
Rolling Off a Log

Key of F
Munster Lass

Key of Am
Brisk Young Lads
Coleraine
Jefferson and Liberty
Rakes of Clonmel
Tenpenny Bit

Key of Em
Happy to Meet, Sorry to Part
Lanigan's Ball
Swallowtail Jig

LIST OF ALTERNATE TITLES

For:	See, in this collection:
Acrobat's Hornpipe	Spitfire Reel
Ap Shenkin	The Tempest
Apex Reel	Gaspé Reel
Atlanta Hornpipe	Batchelder's Reel
Auntie Mary	Cock o' the North
Baie St. Paul	Set de la Baie St. Paul
Barbary Bell	St. Patrick's Day in the Morning
Barmaid	Judy's Reel
Belle Catharine	Come Dance and Sing
Belle of Lexington	Smith's Reel
Belles of Omagh	Morning Star
Big Ship	Reel à Sherbrooke
Blue Water Hornpipe	Pres. Garfield's Hornpipe
Boil the Kettle Early	Piper's Lass
Boston Fancy	Lady Walpole's Reel
Boy in the Boat	Ships are Sailing
Boys of the Lough	Rakes of Clonmel
Boys of Wexford	Snowy-Breasted Pearl
Buffalo Breakdown	Pigtown Fling
Bugle Quickstep	Lady on the Boat
Bummer's Reel	Levantine's Barrel
Bundle and Go	Larry O'Gaff
Bung Your Eye	Brisk Young Lads
Burnt Potato	Little Burnt Potato
Carpenter's Reel	Walker Street
Coachroad to Sligo	Blackthorn Stick
Dance des Sutins	Off She Goes
Daniel O'Connor	Larry O'Gaff
Dusty Miller	Miller's Reel
Father O'Flynn	Top of Cork Road
Galop de Malbie	Mackilmoyle
Gobby O	Jefferson and Liberty
Great Eastern Reel	La Grondeuse
High Road to Linton	Jenny's Gone to Linton
Hop Along Sally	Pigtown Fling
Humours of Whiskey	Larry O'Gaff
Jamie Allen	Jimmy Allen
Joan's Placket	Cock o' the North
John Brennan's Reel	La Grondeuse
John McNeil	Big John McNeil
Ladies' Triumph	Farewell to Whiskey
Lewis Bridal Song	Mairi's Wedding
Little Beggarman	Red Haired Boy
Little Old Man	Old French

For:	See, in this collection:
Lone Appendicitis	Constitution Hornpipe
Maid Behind the Bar	Judy's Reel
Manchester Hornpipe	Rickett's Hornpipe
Mary the Maid	Brisk Young Lads
Massai's Favorite	Lady Walpole's Reel
Merry Blacksmith	Paddy on the Railroad
Merry Soldier	Lamplighter's Hornpipe
Newmarried Couple	Joys of Wedlock
Over the River to Charley's	New Rigged Ship
Pea Soup Reel	Woodchopper's Reel
Persian Dance	Galopede
Picking up Sticks	Kitty McGee
Pigeon on the Gate	Swallowtail Reel
Planxty Maggie Brown	Maggie Brown's Favorite
Portsmouth Hornpipe	Fireman's Reel
Protestant Boys	Lillibulero
Quigley's Reel	Batchelder's Reel
Rambler's Hornpipe	Old French
Red Stocking	Saddle the Pony
Reel des Moissoneurs	Irish-American Reel
Reel du Pê cheur	Democratic Rage
Rollicking Irishman	Top of Cork Road
Roaring Jelly	Smash the Windows
Rosebud Reel	Mountain Ranger
Rural Felicity	Haste to the Wedding
Rustic Dance	Off She Goes
St. Vincent's Hornpipe	Vinton's Hornpipe
Silver Spire	La Grondeuse
Simple Gifts	'Tis the Gift to be Simple
Snoring Gobeil	Ronfleuse Gobeil
Stoney Point	Pigtown Fling
Stony Steps Hornpipe	Red Lion
Sweet Biddy Daly	Irishman's Heart to the Ladies
Temperance Reel	Teetotaler's Reel
There Came a Young Man	Brisk Young Lads
Three Little Drummers	Tenpenny Bit
Timour the Tartar	Peter Street
Traveler's Reel	Walker Street
Uncle Jim	Steamboat Quickstep
Vielle Fille	L'Oiseau Bleu
Washington Quickstep	Steamboat Quickstep
Yarmouth Reel	Galopede
Young America Hornpipe	Farewell to Whiskey

ORIGINAL ORDER OF TUNES, 1983
Jigs, followed by Reels, Hornpipes and Marches

Broken Lantern	C		Hundred Pipers	A
Blackthorn Stick	G		Cock o' the North	A
Kitty McGee	D		Rolling Off a Log	C
The Tempest	G		Lanigan's Ball	Em
Rory O'More	A		Bell's Favorite	D
Connaught Man's Rambles	D		Munster Buttermilk	G
Saint Lawrence Jig	D		Saint Patrick's Day in the Morning	G
Hullichan Jig	G		Soldier's Cloak	D
Maple Leaf Jig	G		Maggie Brown's Favorite	G
Tenpenny Bit	Am		Swallowtail Jig	Em
Smash the Windows	D		Portland Fancy	A
Jefferson and Liberty	Am		Road to Boston	D
Irishman's Heart to the Ladies	A		Mairi's Wedding	G
Lillibulero	A		Earl of Mansfield	A
Coleraine	Am		Red Lion	Bb
Brisk Young Lads	Am		Finnegan's Wake	D
Saddle the Pony	G		Jenny's Gone to Linton	A
Joys of Wedlock	G		O'Donnell Abu	G
Jackson's Fancy	D		My Love's But a Lassie	D
Blackberry Quadrille	D		Rakes of Mallow	G
Steamboat Quickstep	A		Roddy McCorley	D
Muckin' o' Geordie's Byre	D		Jimmy Allen	G
Happy to Meet, Sorry to Part	Em		Snowy-Breasted Pearl	A
Little Burnt Potato	D		Meeting of the Waters	A
Paddy Whack	A		All the Way to Galway	D
Rock Valley	C		Rose Tree	D
Come Up the Back Stairs	G		Galopede	G
Shandon Bells	D		Lardner's Reel	A
Cattle in the Crops	D		Prince William	A
Haste to the Wedding	D		Deerfoot	F
Rakes of Clonmel	Am		Maguinnis' Delight	F
Larry O'Gaff	G		Morpeth Rant	D
Top of Cork Road	D		Come Dance and Sing	D
Munster Lass	F		High Level Hornpipe	Bb
Off She Goes	D		Paddy on the Turnpike	Gm
Stool of Repentance	A		Paddy on the Railroad	D
Bonnie Dundee	G		Poppy Leaf Hornpipe	G
Lady on the Boat	D		Corn Rigs	D
Kenmure's Up and Awa'	A		Starr Label Reel	A
Starry Night for a Ramble	D		Fireman's Reel	A
New Rigged Ship	D		Ships are Sailing	Em

NEW ENGLAND FIDDLER'S REPERTOIRE

Tune	Key	Tune	Key
Irish-American Reel	F	Pigtown Fling	G
Mason's Apron	A	Old French	D
Spitfire Reel	Bb	Swallowtail Reel	Em
Far from Home	G	Staten Island Hornpipe	D
Swinging on a Gate	G	Batchelder's Reel	F
Teetotaler's Reel	G	Sheehan's Reel	G
Walker Street	G	Red-Haired Boy	A
Miller's Reel	A	Big John McNeil	A
Smith's Reel	D	Farewell to Whiskey	G
Wind That Shakes the Barley	D	Allie Crocker's Reel	D
Opera Reel	D	Snowflake Hornpipe	A
Speed the Plow	A	Jock Tamson's Hornpipe	D
Scotch Hornpipe	D	Rickett's Hornpipe	D
Chorus Jig	D	Saint Anne's Reel	D
Green Mountain Petronella	G	Hull's Victory	F
Piper's Lass	D	La Bastringue	D
Petronella	D	Gandy Dancer's Reel	D
President Garfield's Hornpipe	Bb	Indian Reel	G
President Grant's Hornpipe	Bb	Levantine's Barrel	G
President Lincoln's Hornpipe	A	Mother's Reel	C
Constitution Hornpipe	F	Little Judique	D
Democratic Rage Hornpipe	Bb	Jacques Cartier	D
White Cockade	G	Growling Old Man and Woman	Am
Crooked Stovepipe	G	Woodchopper's Reel	D
Money Musk	A	Mackilmoyle	D
Lamplighter's Hornpipe	A	Chatagee Reel	G
Miss McCleod's Reel	G	Snowshoer's Reel	F
Lady Walpole's Reel	Bb	Peter Street	A
Green Fields of America	G	Ronfleuse Gobeil	D
Ross's Reel #4	F	Gaspé Reel	D
Judy's Reel	D	La Grondeuse	D
Belles of Tipperary	D	Les Fraises et les Framboises	G
Inimitable Reel	G	Glise à Sherbrooke	G
Forester's Hornpipe	D	La Toque Bleue	G
Fisher's Hornpipe	F	Set de la Baie St. Paul	D
Vinton's Hornpipe	Bb	Reel des Jeunes Mariés	D
Devil's Dream	A	Pays de Haut	D
Quindaro Hornpipe	G	L'Oiseau Bleu	D
Durang's Hornpipe	D	Reel de Montréal	G
Flowers of Edinburgh	G	Reel de Ti-Jean	D
Mountain Ranger	Bb	Gay Gordons	A
Morning Star	G	Il est Né	G
Cincinnati Hornpipe	D	'Tis the Gift to be Simple	G

All the Way to Galway

Allie Crocker's Reel

Lawrence Grogan, c. 1725

NEW ENGLAND FIDDLER'S REPERTOIRE

La Bastringue

Batchelder's Reel

Bell's Favorite

Belles of Tipperary

Big John McNeil

Peter Milne

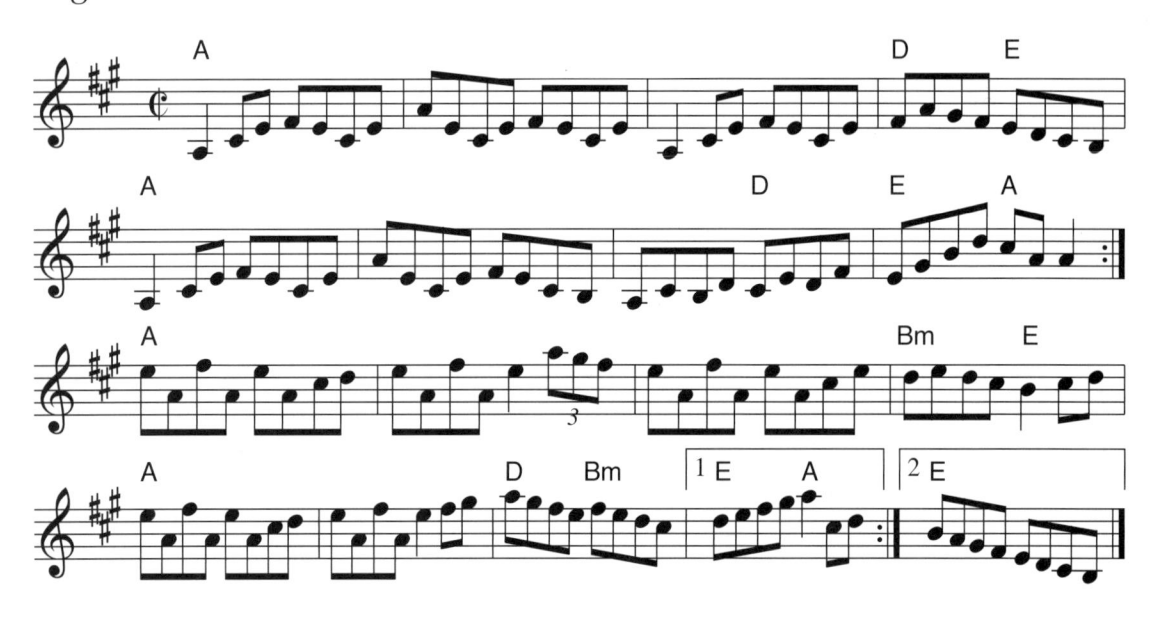

Blackberry Quadrille

Blackthorn Stick

Bonnie Dundee

Brisk Young Lads

Tom Doyle, c. 1883

Broken Lantern

Cattle in the Crops

Jim Magill

Chatagee Reel

Chorus Jig

Cincinnati Hornpipe

Cock o' the North

NEW ENGLAND FIDDLER'S REPERTOIRE

Coleraine

Come Dance and Sing

Come Up the Back Stairs

Connaught Man's Rambles

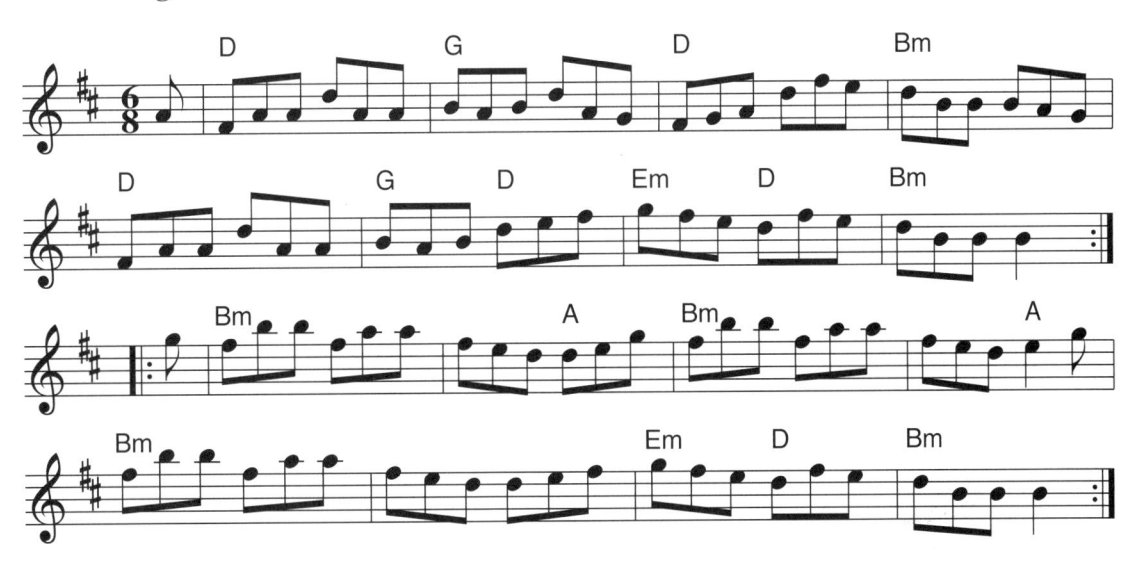

Constitution Hornpipe

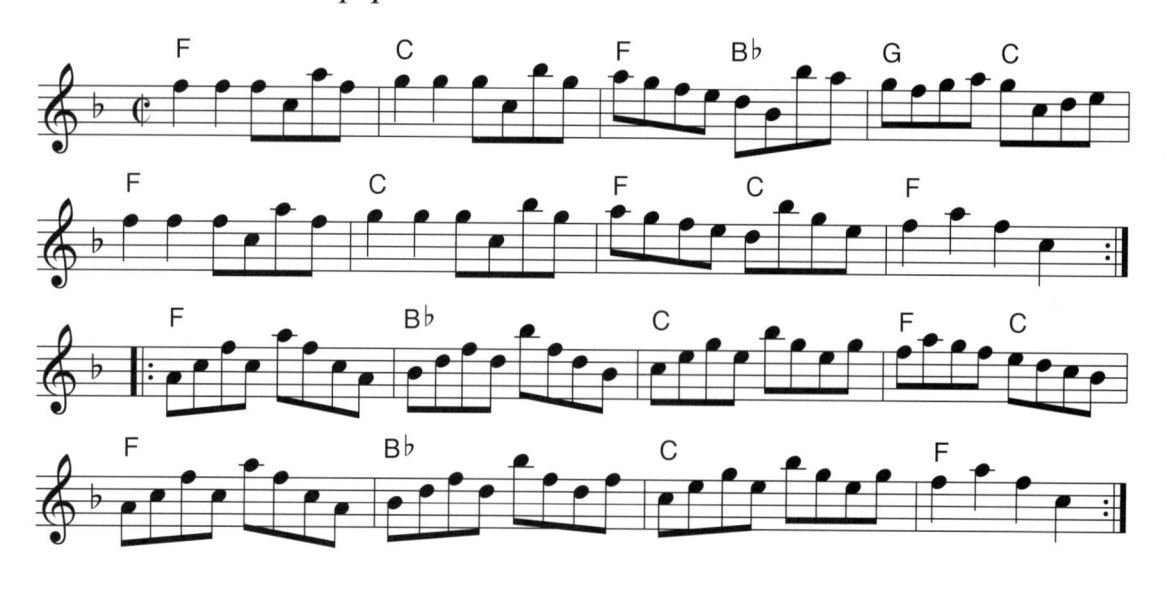

Corn Rigs

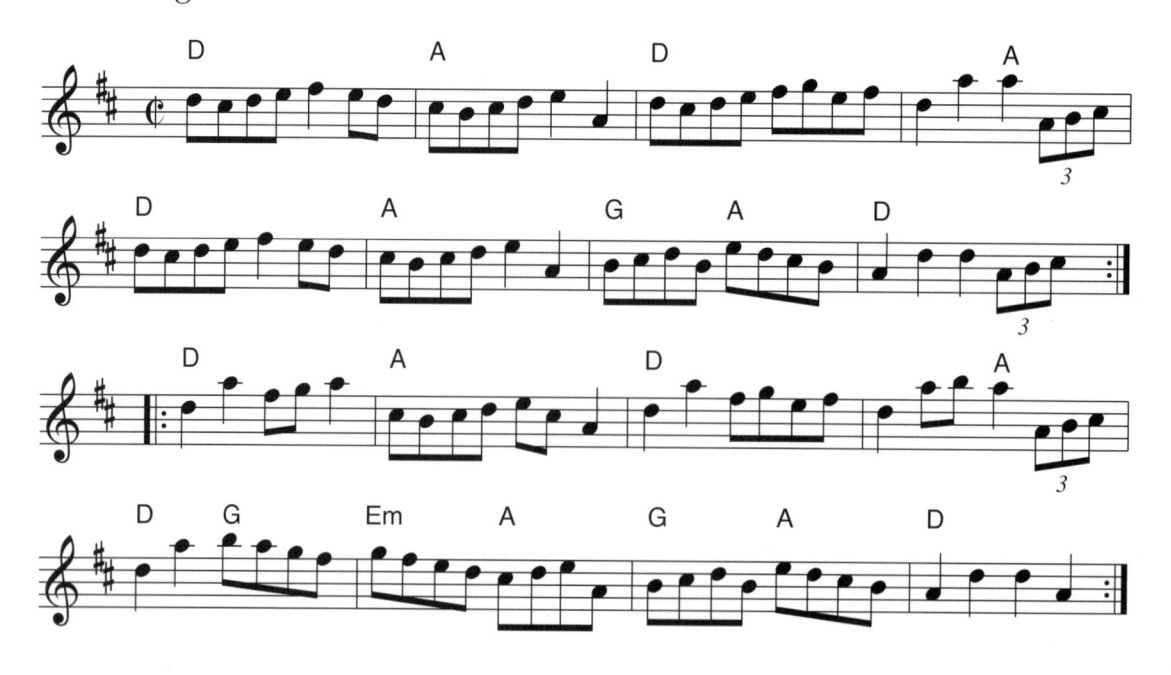

Crooked Stovepipe

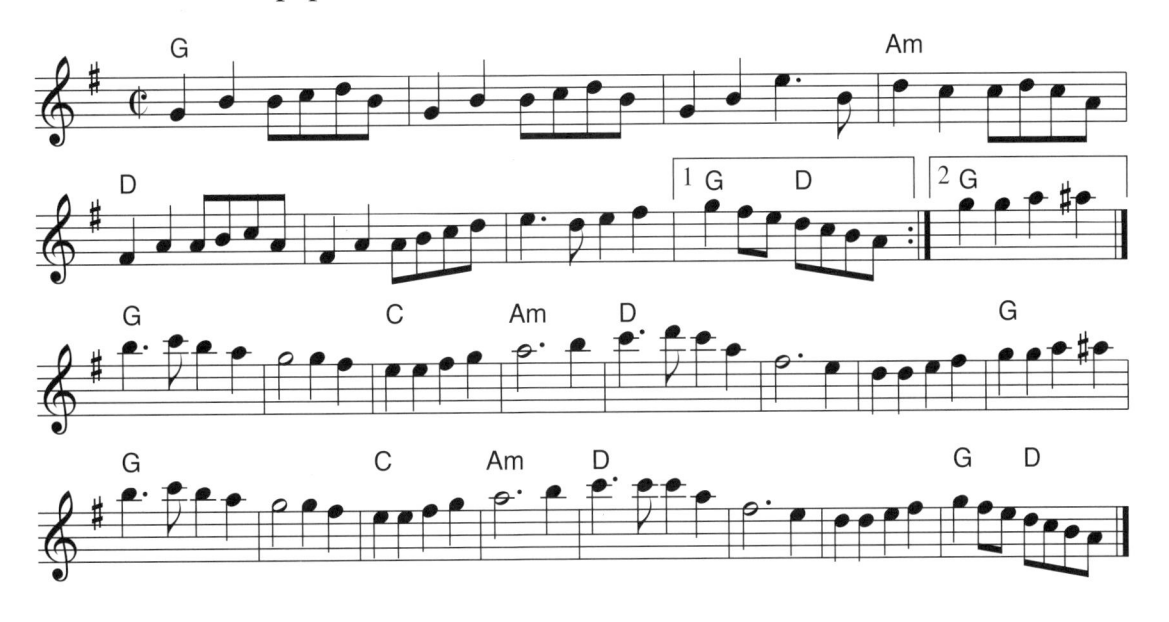

Deerfoot

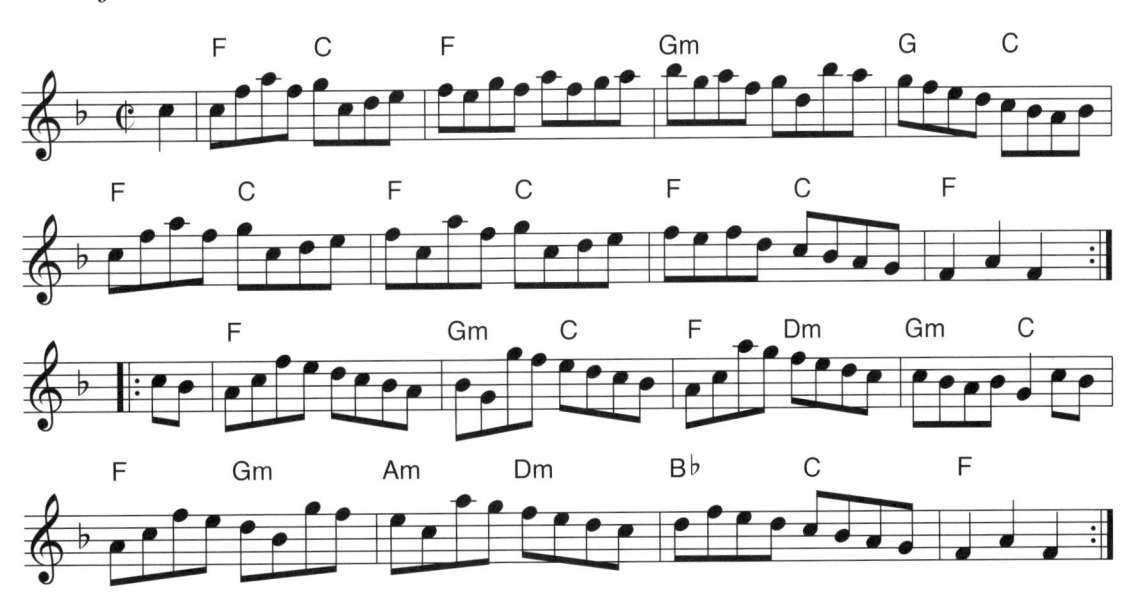

Democratic Rage Hornpipe

Devil's Dream

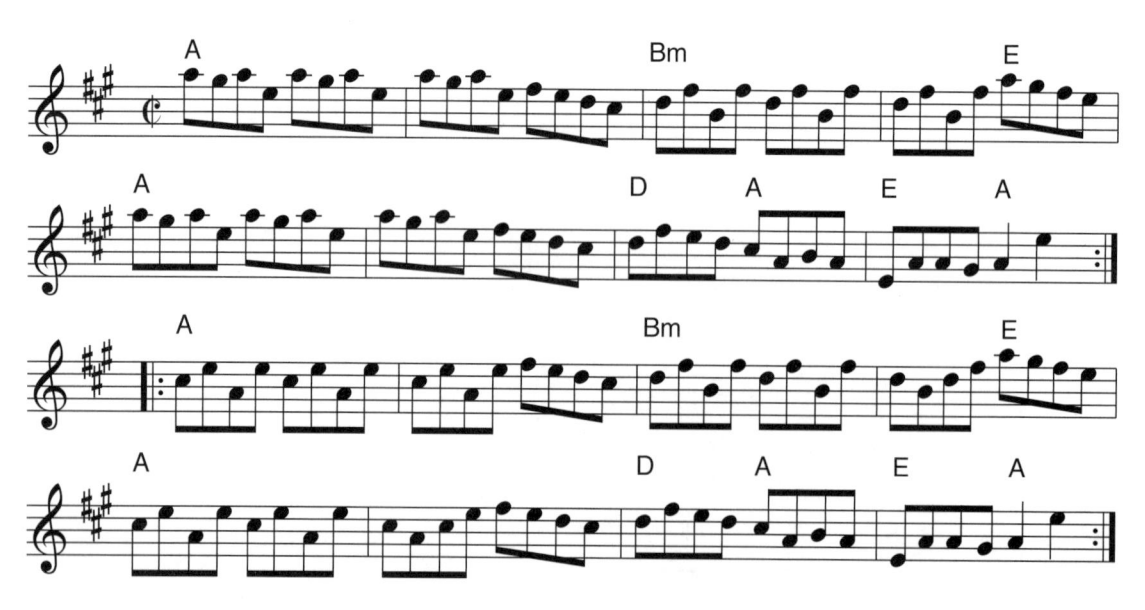

Durang's Hornpipe

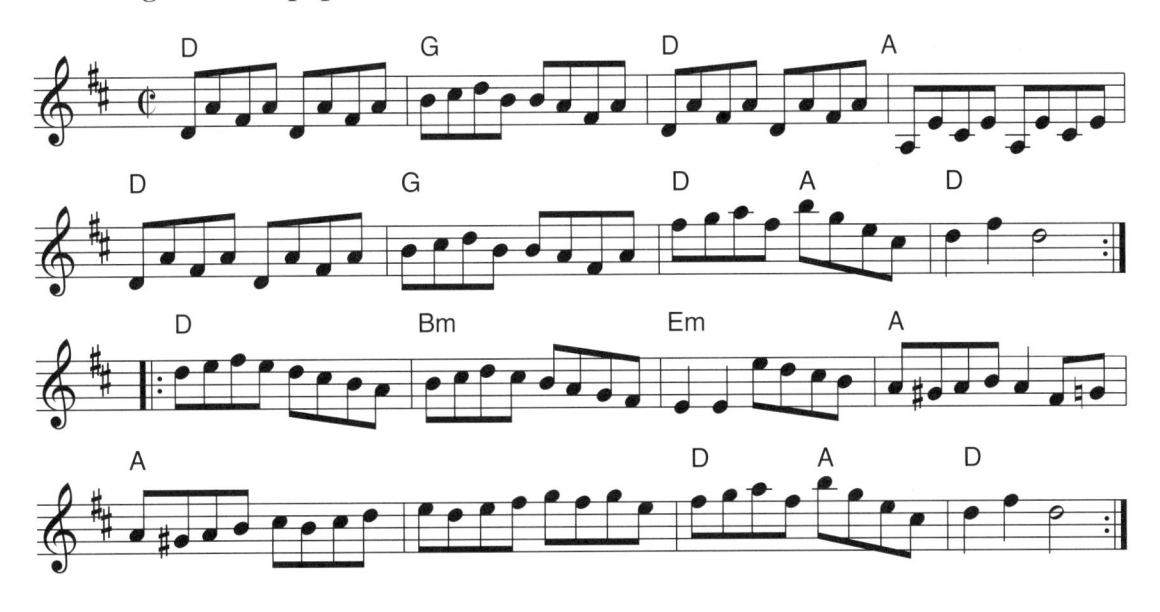

dance in Nelson, N.H.

Earl of Mansfield

J. McEwan

Far From Home

Farewell to Whiskey

Neil Gow, c. 1801

Finnegan's Wake

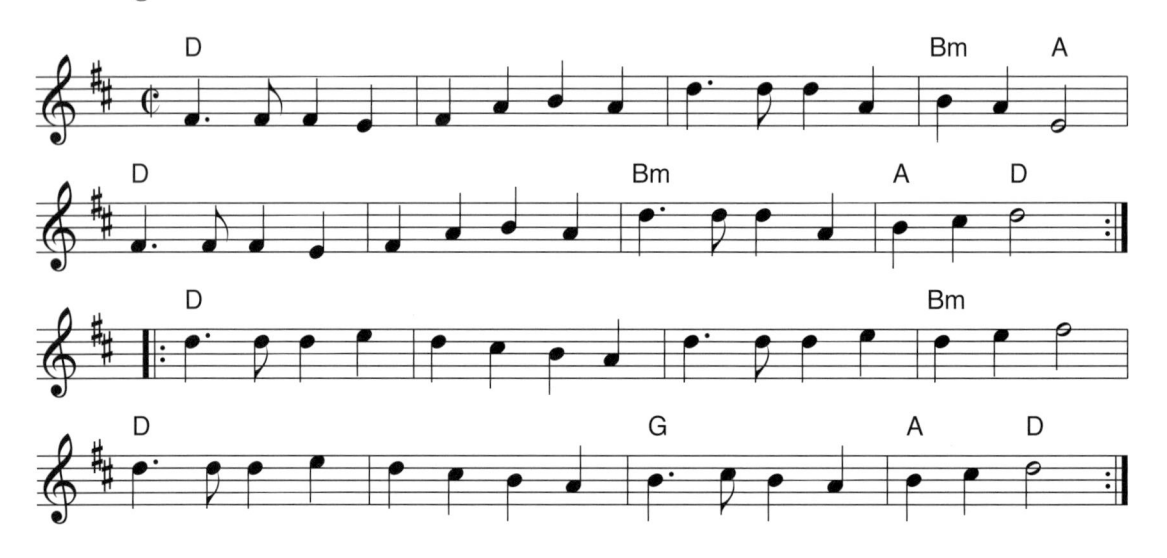

Fireman's Reel

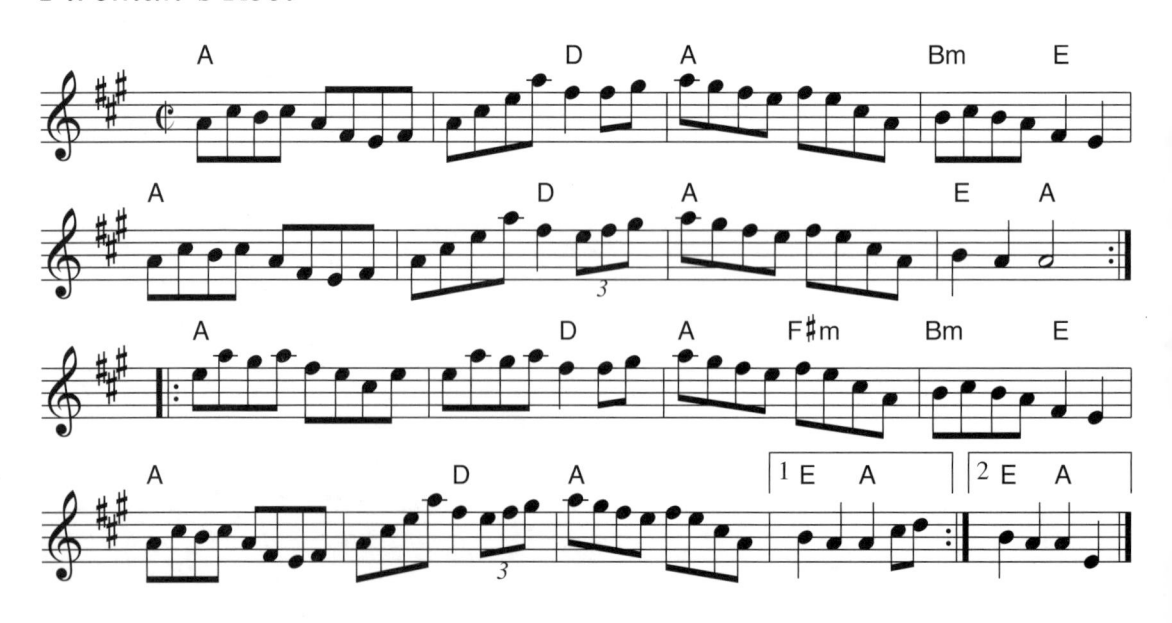

Fisher's Hornpipe

Flowers of Edinburgh

James Oswald, c. 1742

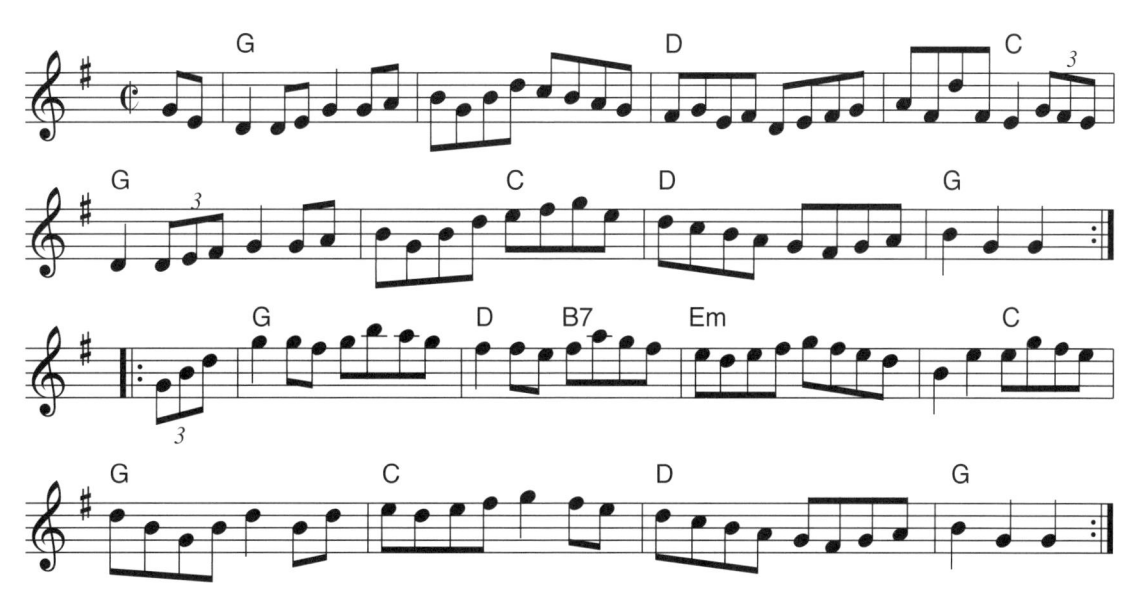

Forester's Hornpipe

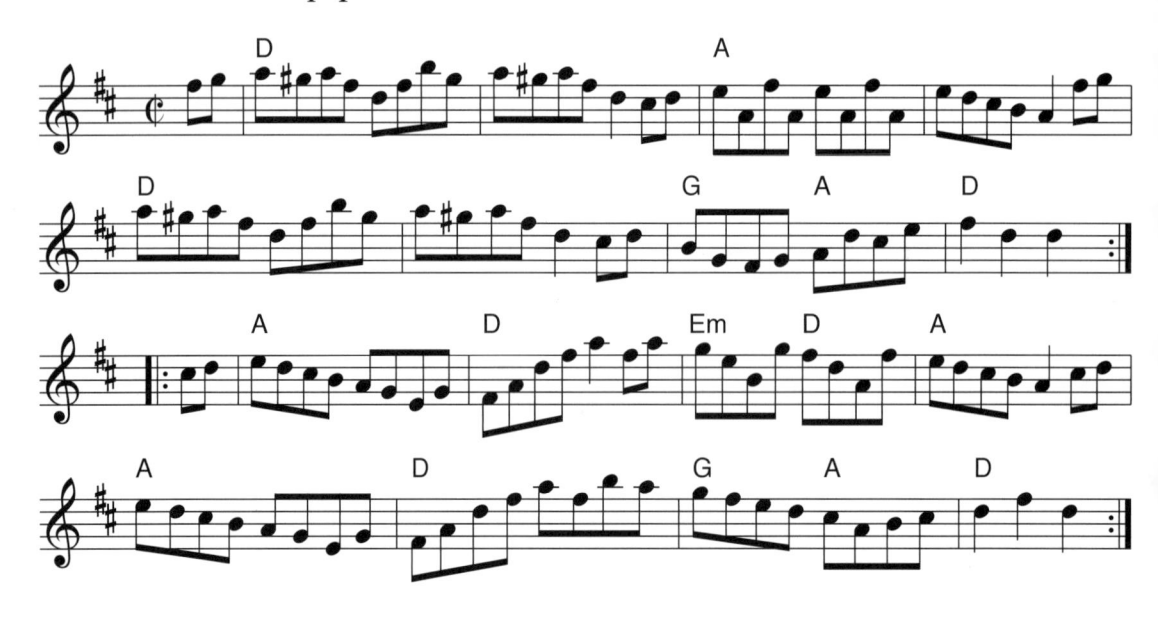

Les Fraises et les Framboises

Galopede

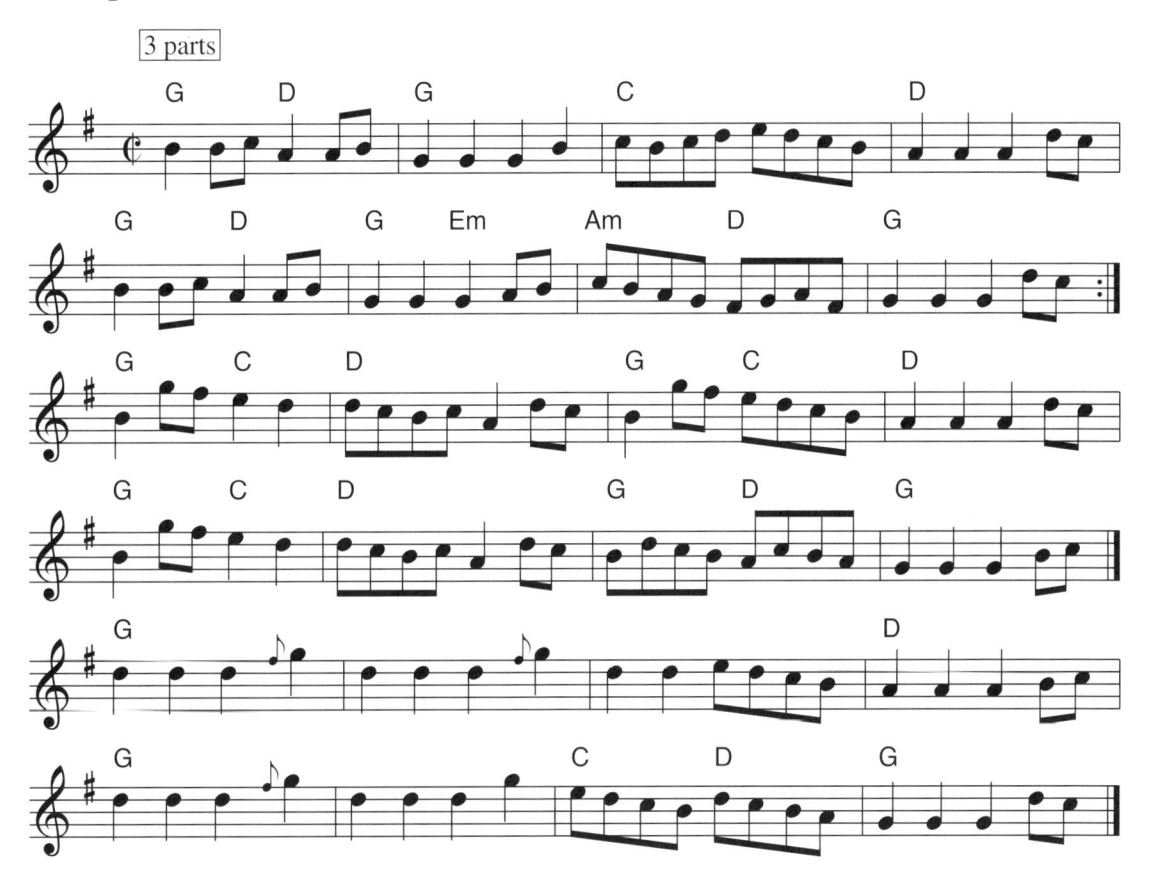

NEW ENGLAND FIDDLER'S REPERTOIRE

Gandy Dancer's Reel

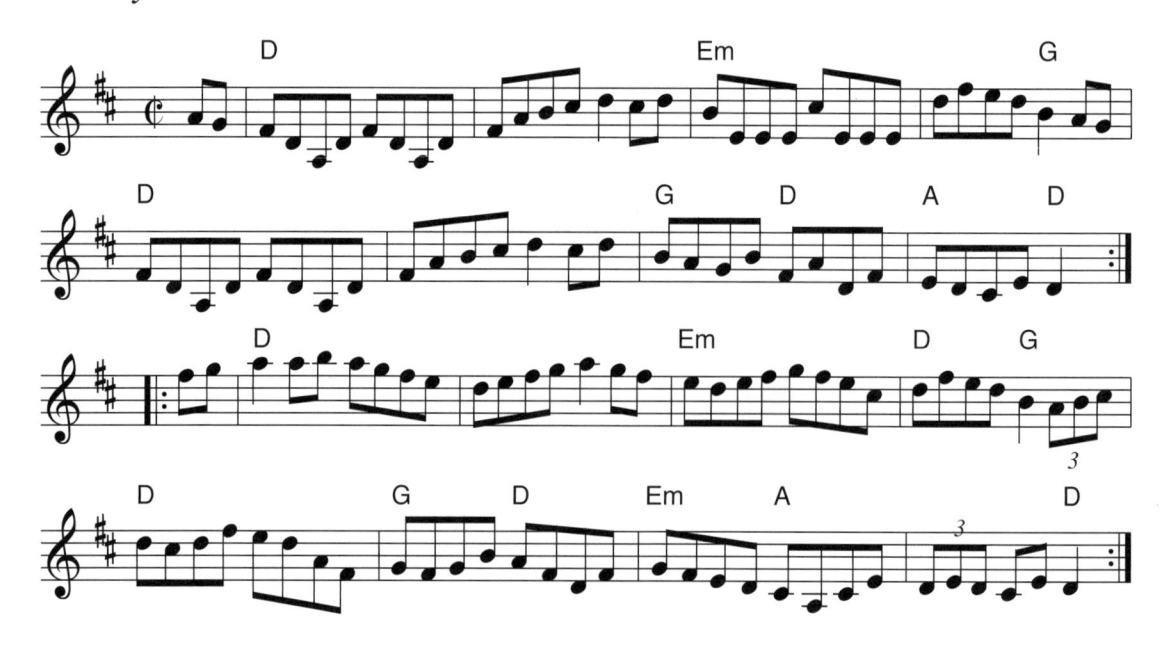

Gaspé Reel

Gay Gordons (couple dance)

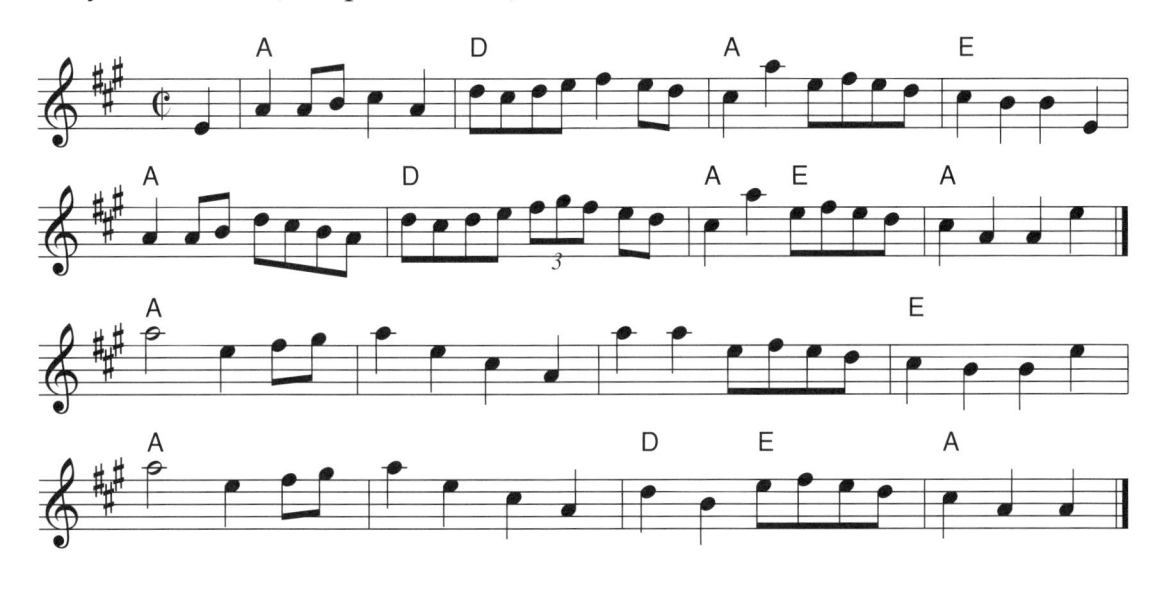

Glise à Sherbrooke

Green Fields of America

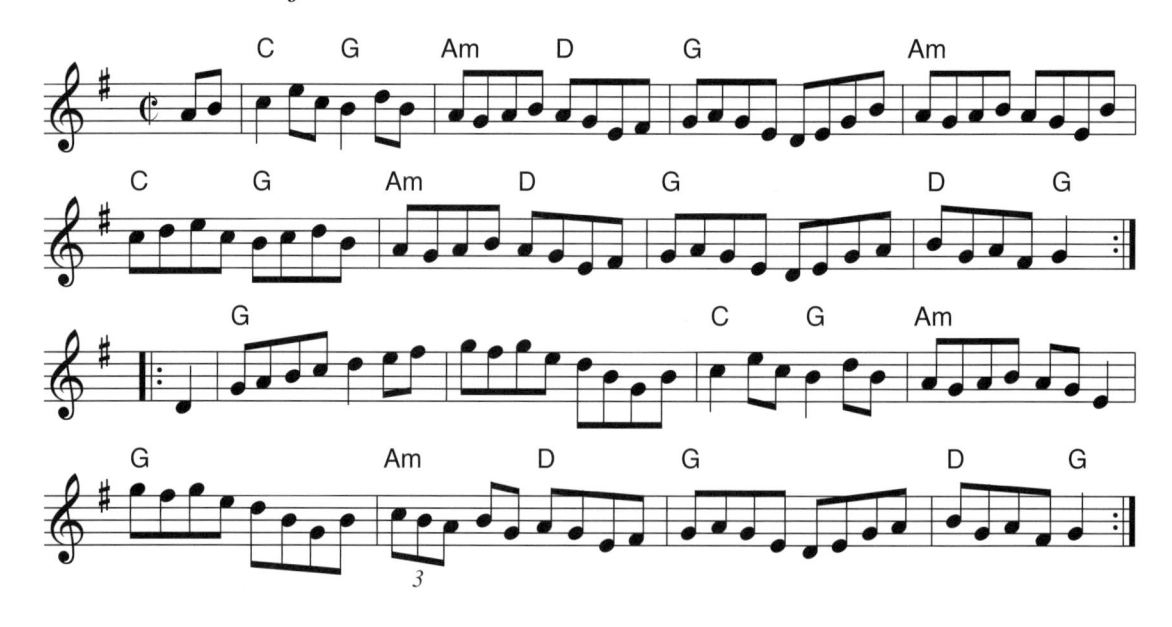

Green Mountain Petronella

La Grondeuse

Growling Old Man and Woman

Happy to Meet, Sorry to Part

Haste to the Wedding

High Level Hornpipe
James Hill, c. 1850

Hull's Victory

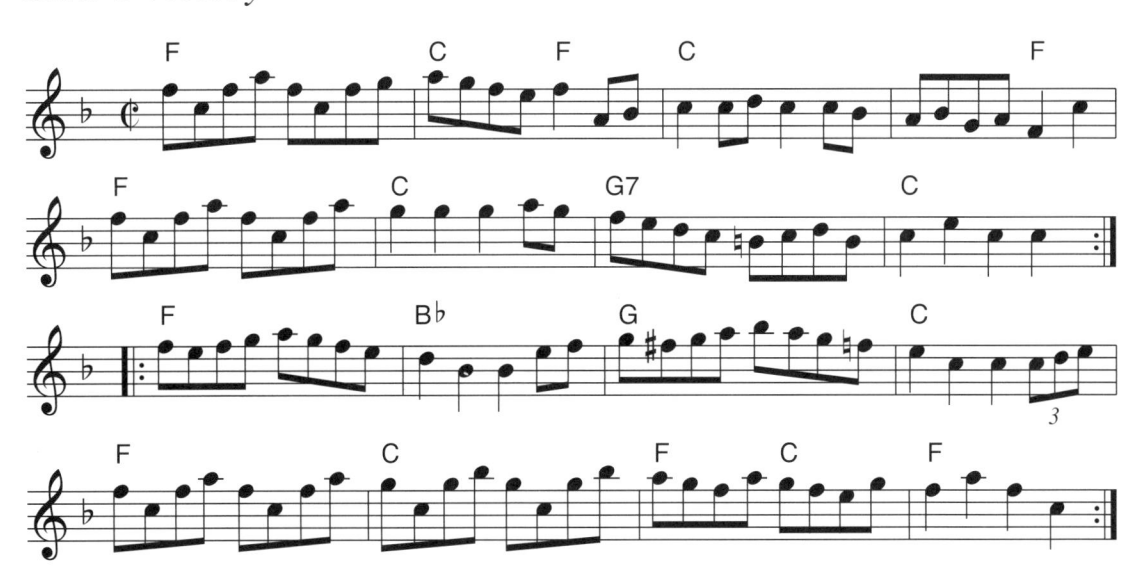

Hullichan Jig

Hundred Pipers

Il est Né

Indian Reel

Inimitable Reel

Irish-American Reel

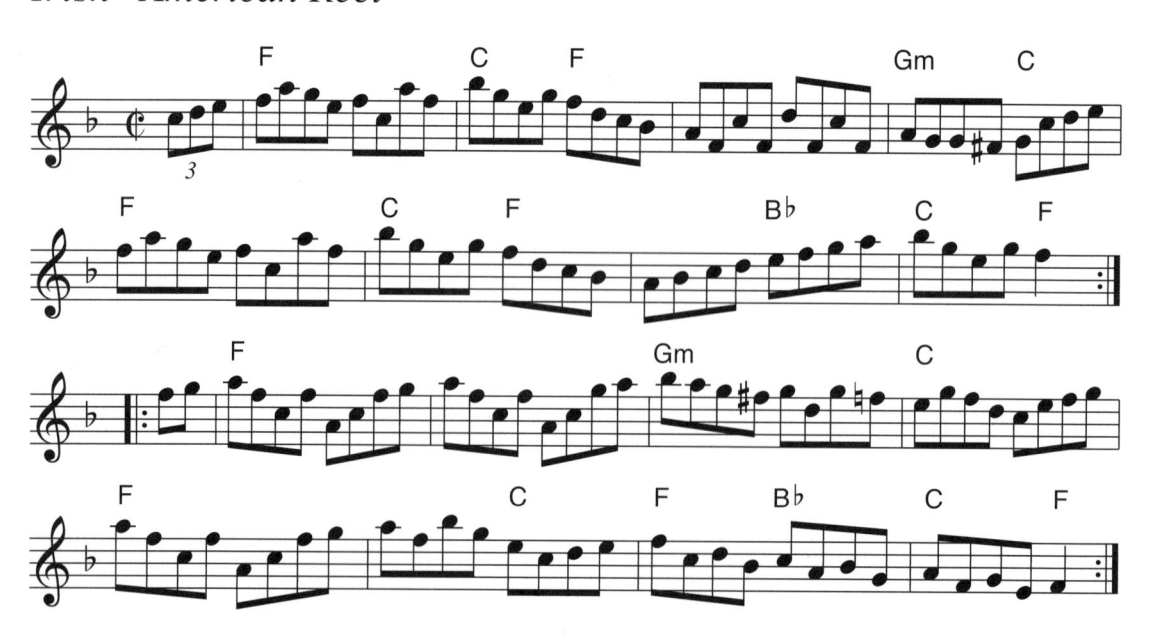

Irishman's Heart to the Ladies

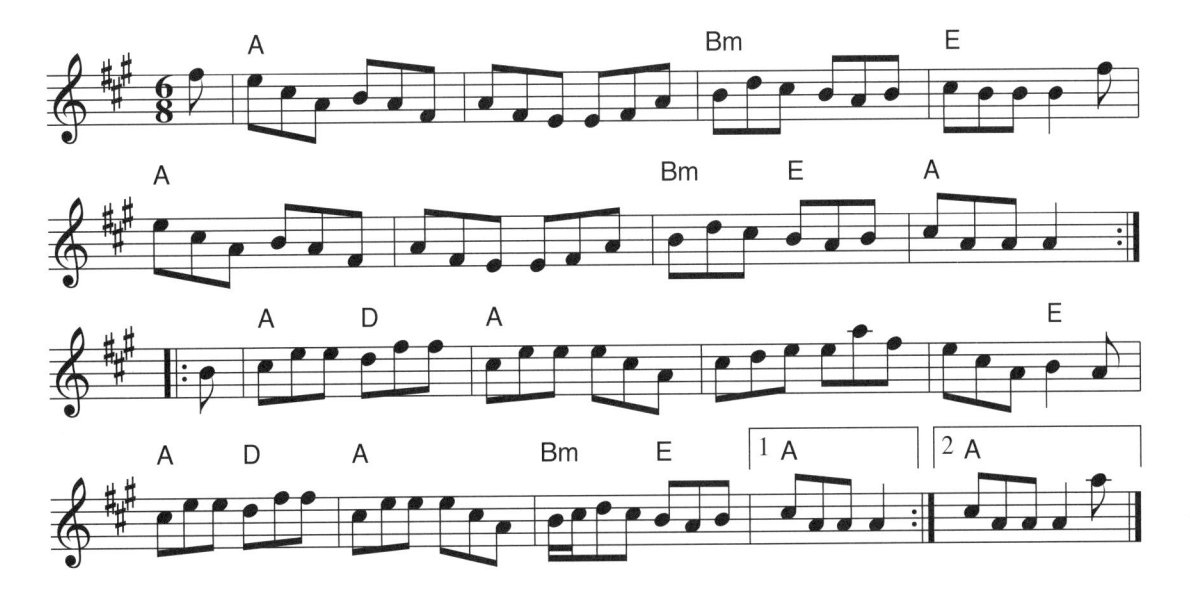

Jackson's Fancy

Jacques Cartier

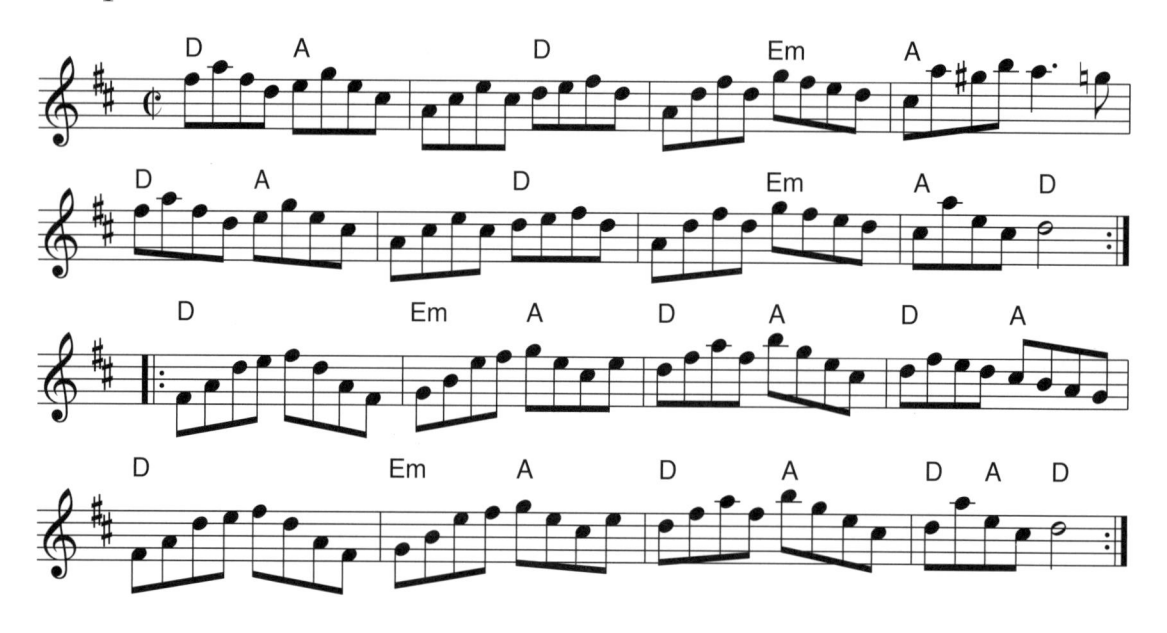

Jefferson and Liberty

Jenny's Gone to Linton

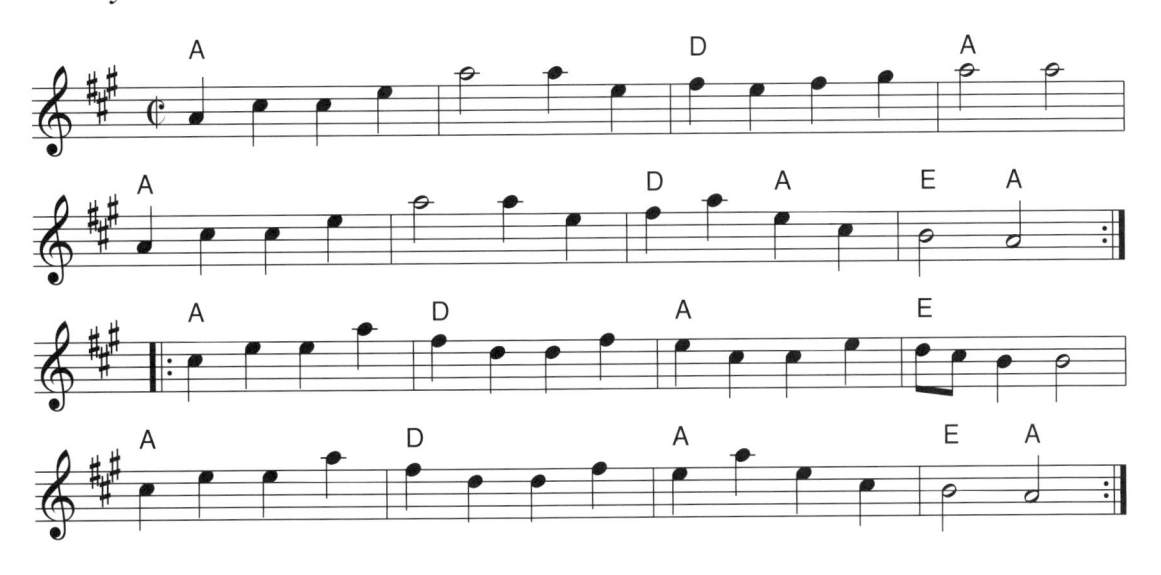

Reel des Jeunes Mariés

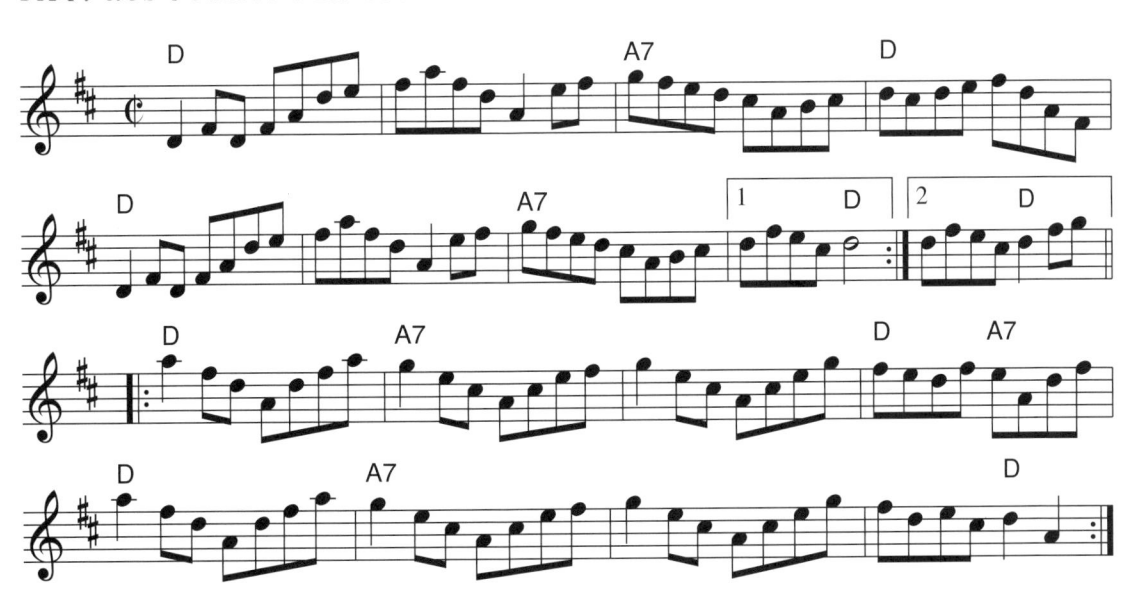

Jimmy Allen

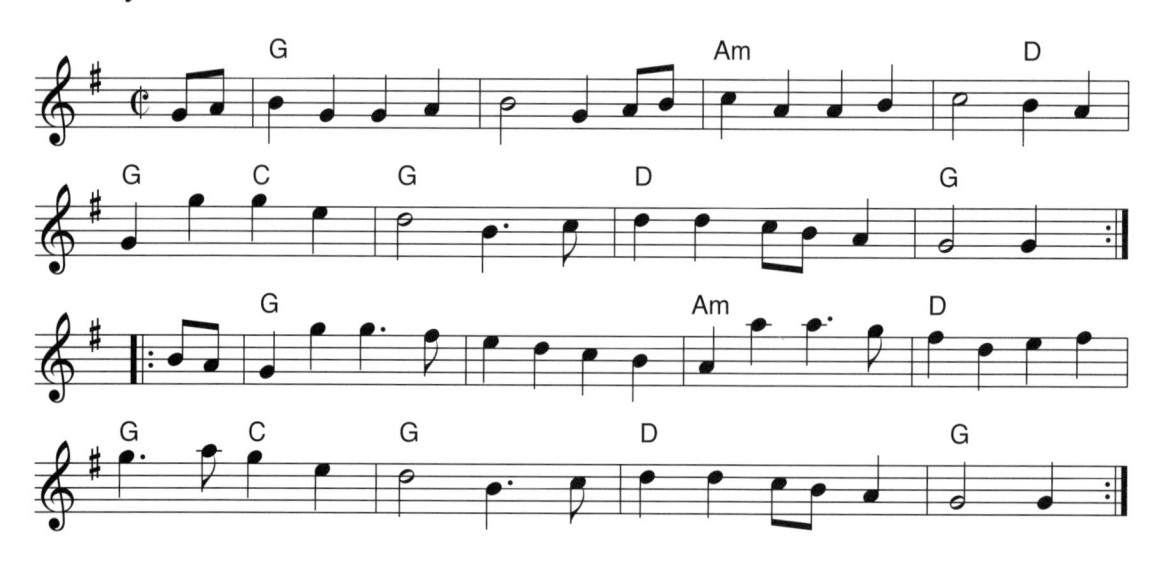

Jock Tamson's Hornpipe

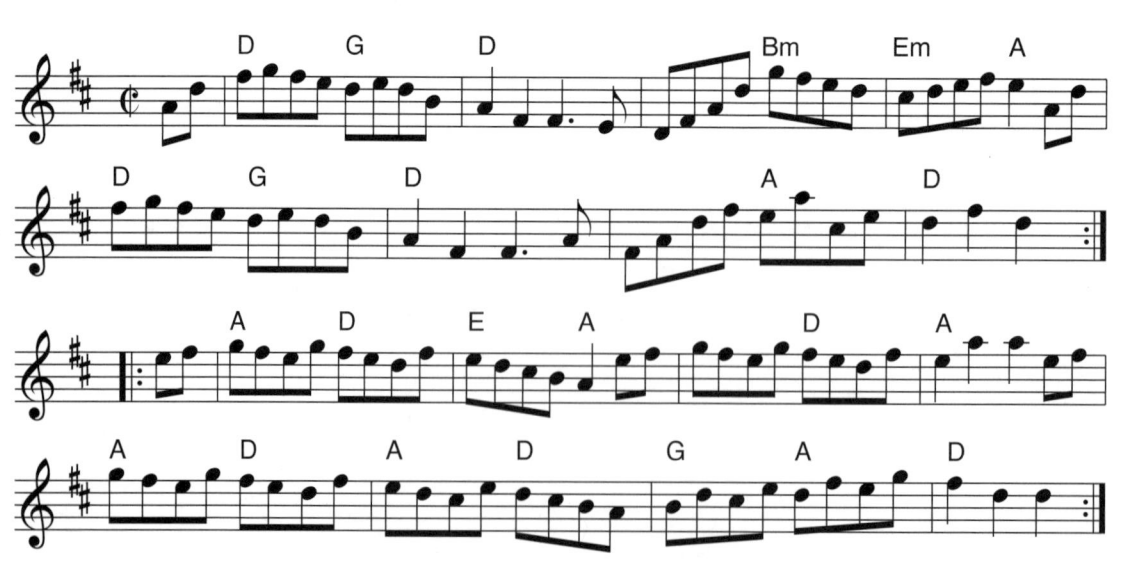

Joys of Wedlock

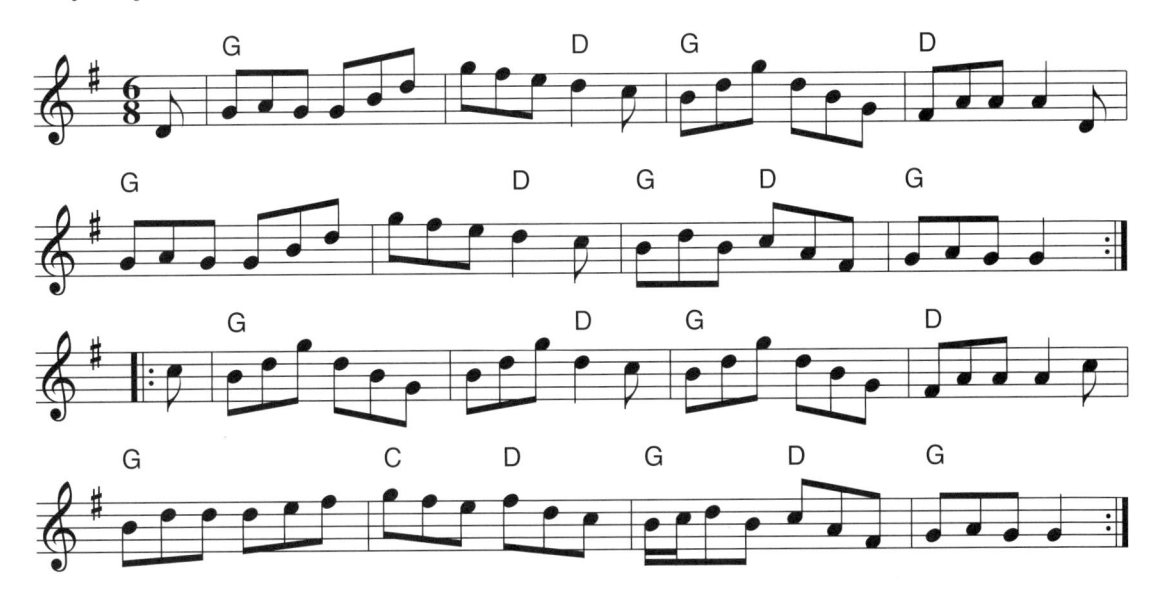

Judy's Reel

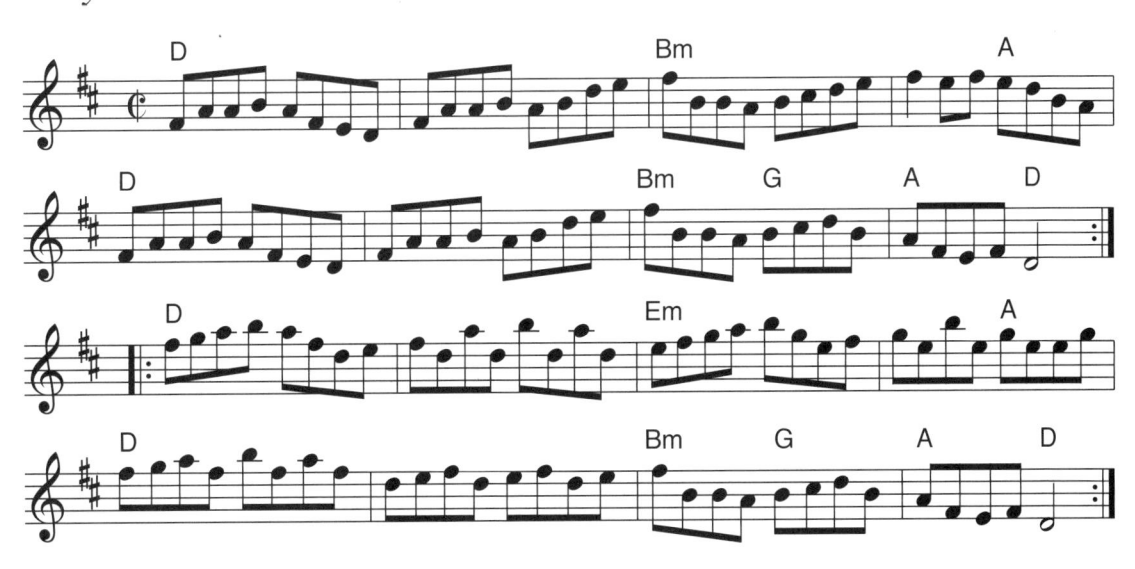

Kenmure's Up and Awa'

Kitty McGee

Lady on the Boat

Lady Walpole's Reel

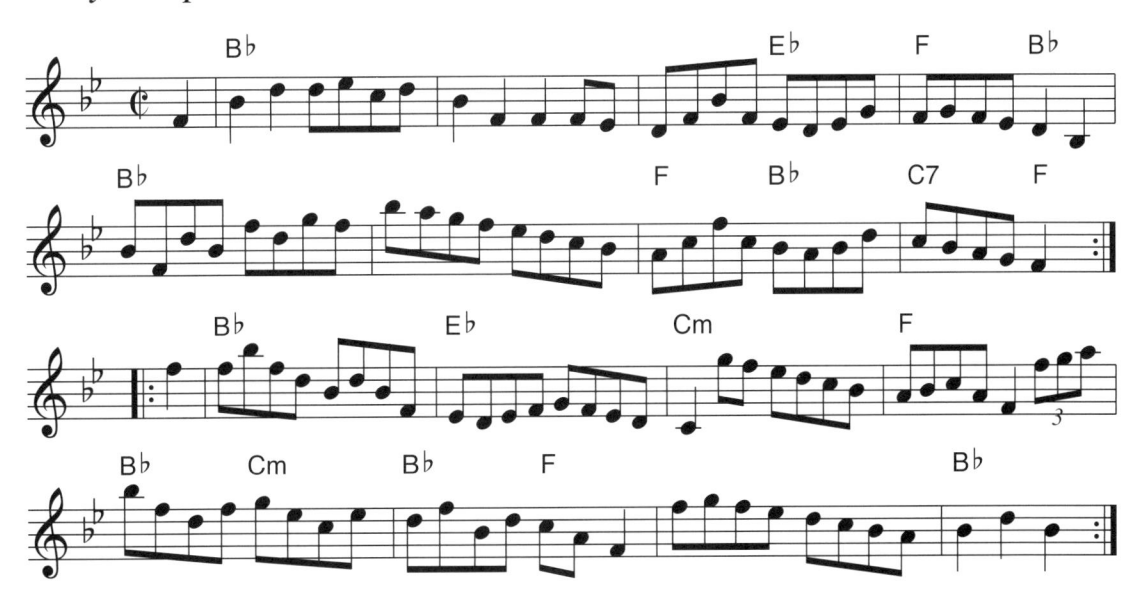

Lamplighter's Hornpipe

Lanigan's Ball

Lardner's Reel

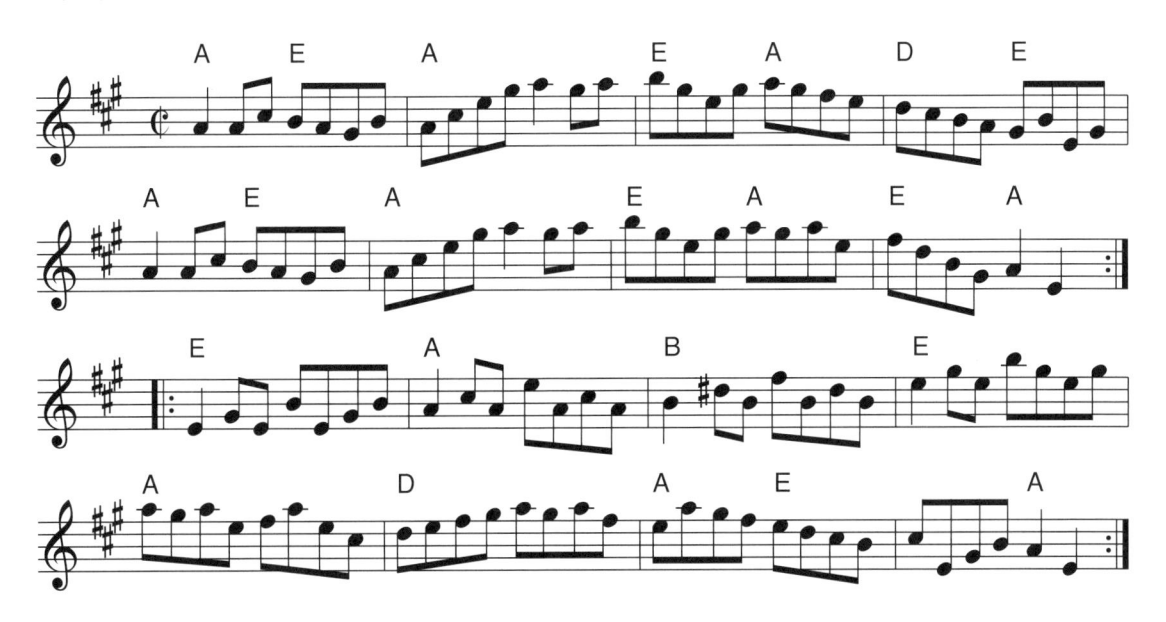

Larry O'Gaff

Levantine's Barrel

Lillibulero

Little Burnt Potato

Little Judique

February 12. Played for a Forestry Meet dance in a barn with a sawdust floor at the University of New Hampshire in Durham. The temperature was 15 degrees below zero.

–Randy Miller, dance diary, 1978

Mackilmoyle

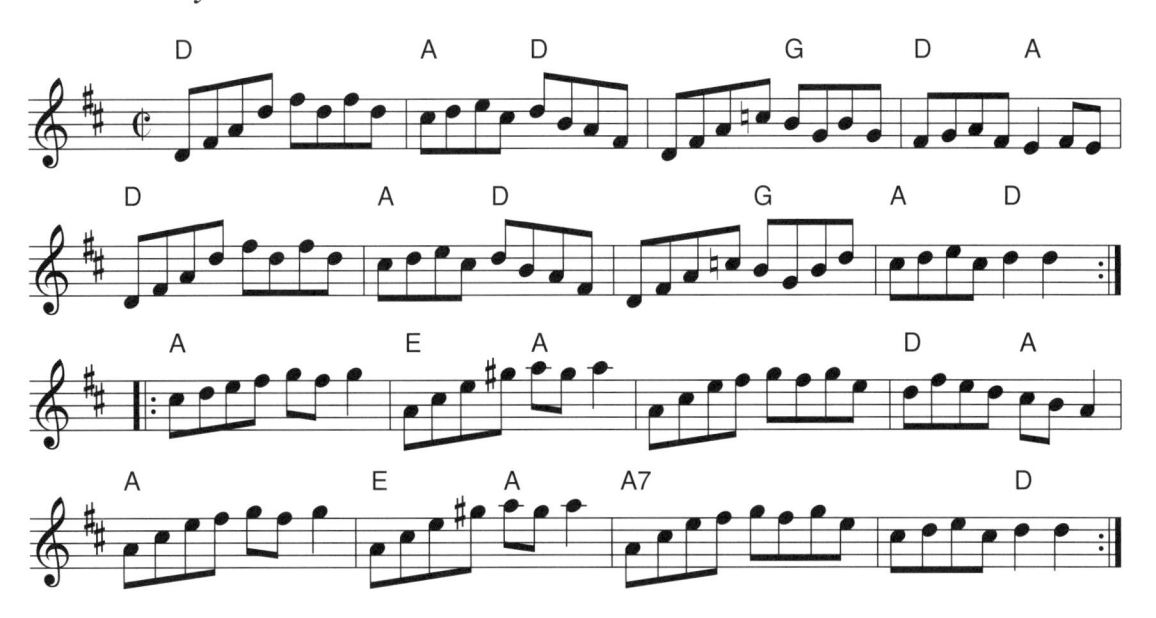

Maggie Brown's Favorite

Nathaniel Gow, c. 1819

Walpole, NH, town hall

NEW ENGLAND FIDDLER'S REPERTOIRE

Maguinnis's Delight

Mairi's Wedding

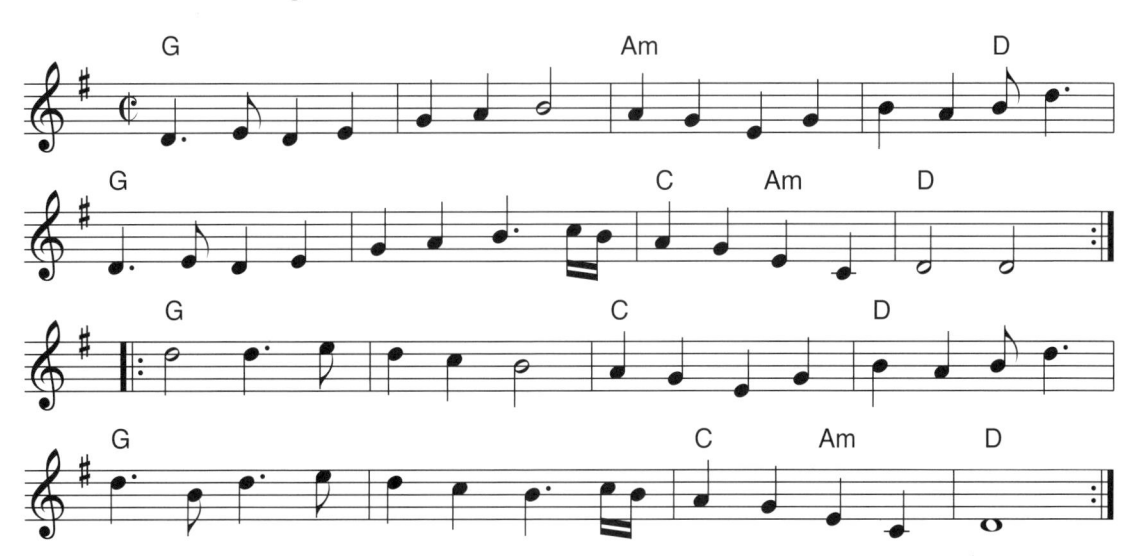

Maple Leaf Jig

Mason's Apron

Meeting of the Waters

Miller's Reel

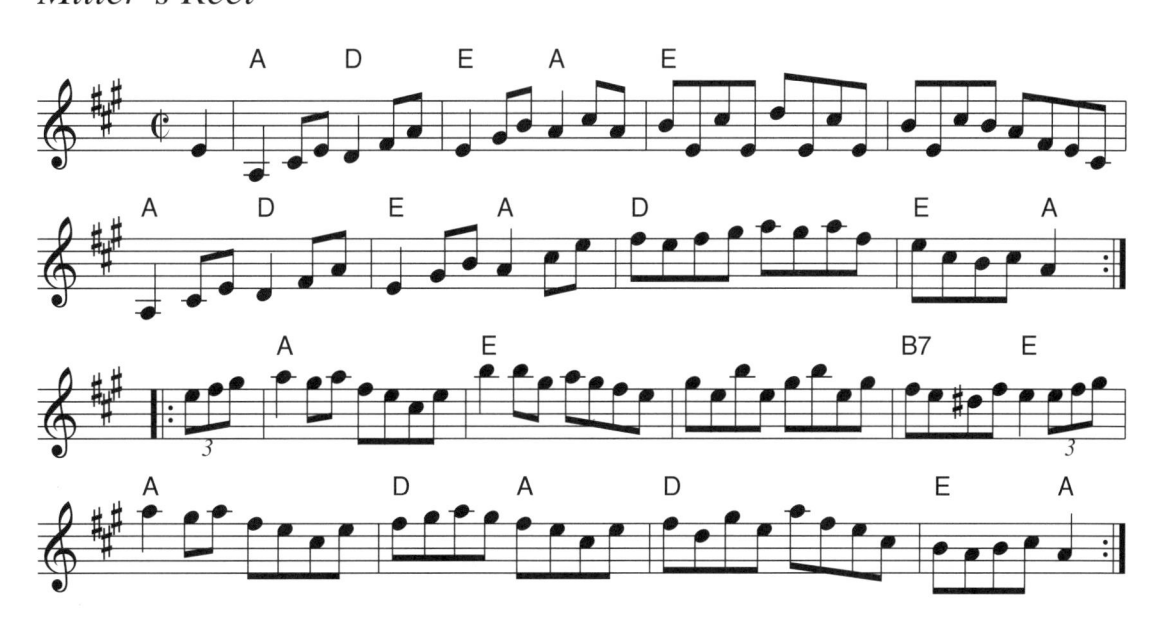

Miss McLeod's Reel

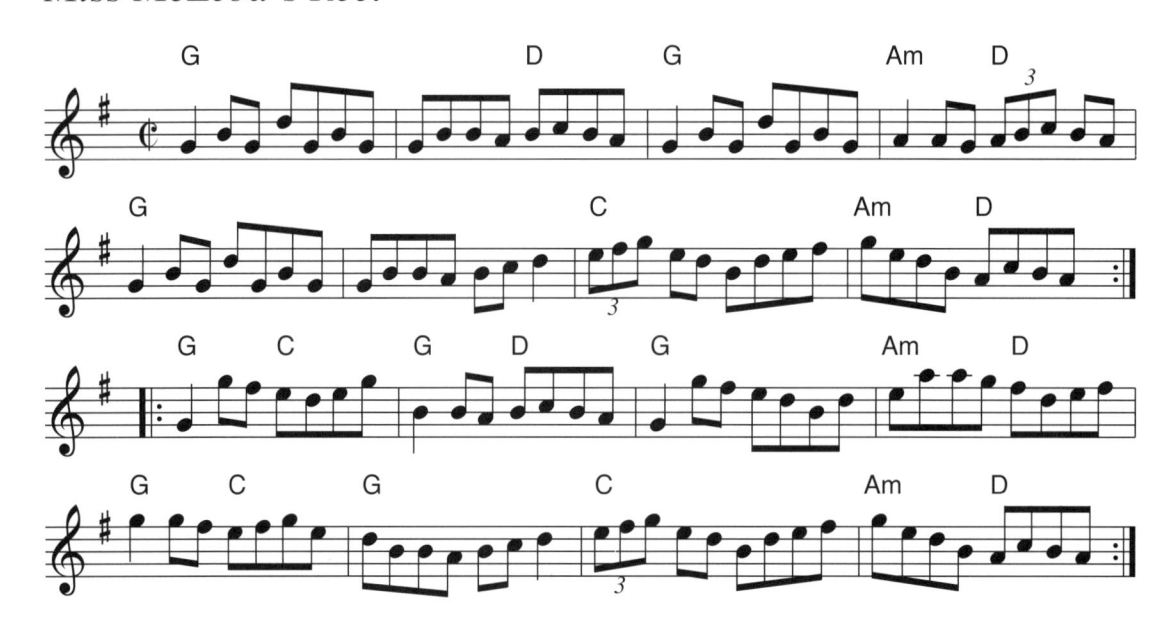

Money Musk

Daniel Dow, c. 1776

3 parts

Alternate B Part

They say that this was first danced on the village green of Moneymusk on the river Don in Aberdeenshire...there have been as many variations on the original tune as there have been fiddlers to play them.
    —Beth Tolman and Ralph Page, *The Country Dance Book*, 1937

Reel de Montréal

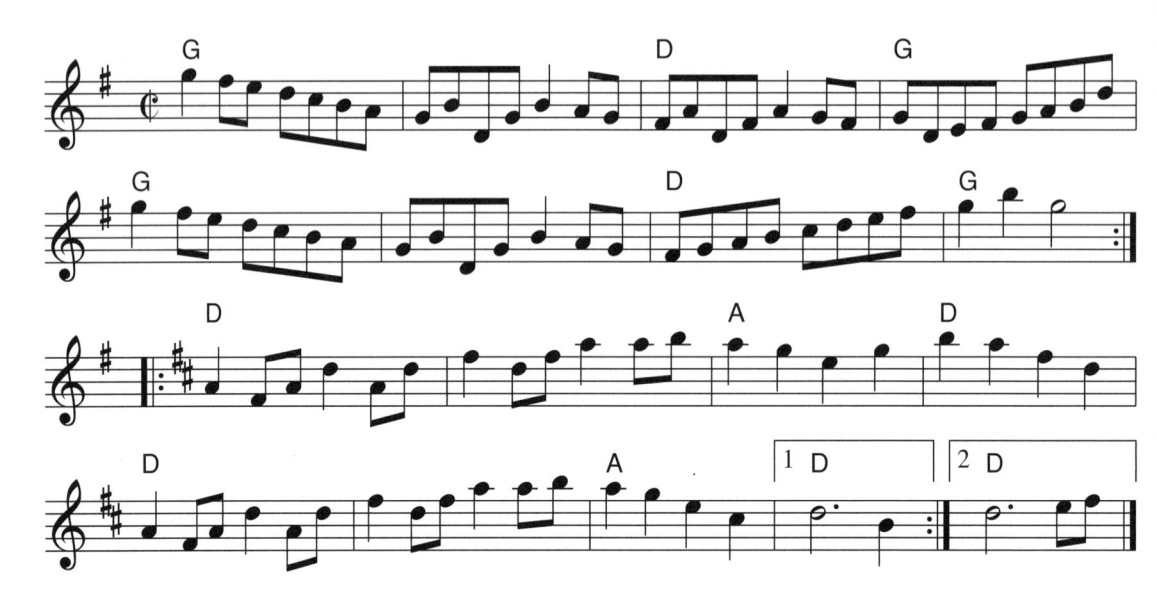

Morning Star

NEW ENGLAND FIDDLER'S REPERTOIRE

Morpeth Rant

William Shields

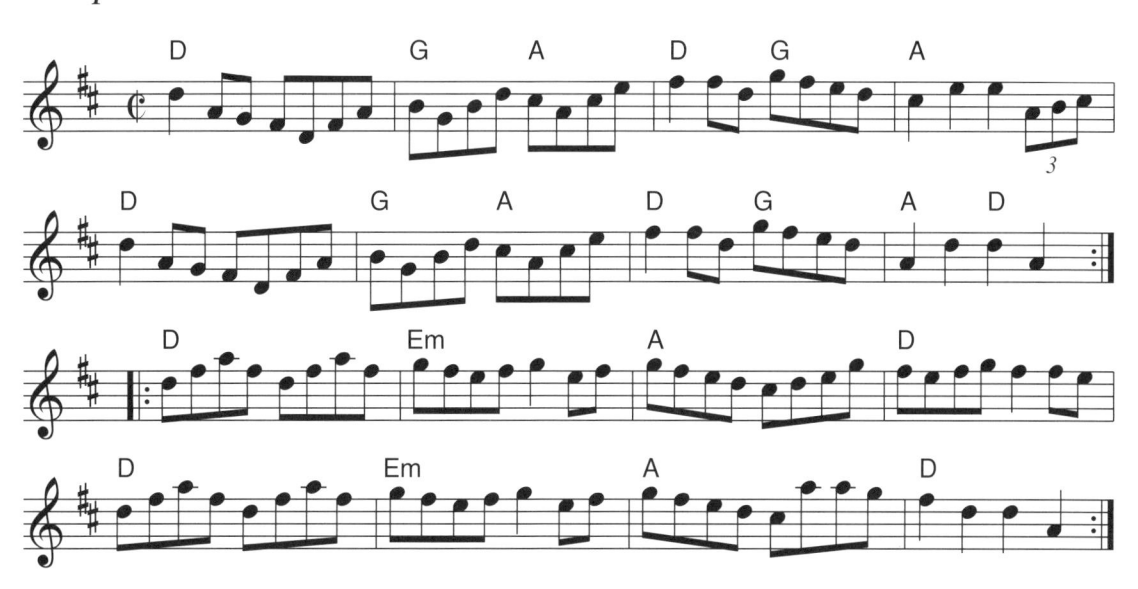

Mother's Reel

Don Messer

[3 parts]

Each melody must have some character or quality that sets it apart from all others, and which makes it usually impossible to be imitated successfully.

–Newt Tolman's definition of good dance music,
Quick Tunes and Good Times, 1972

Mountain Ranger

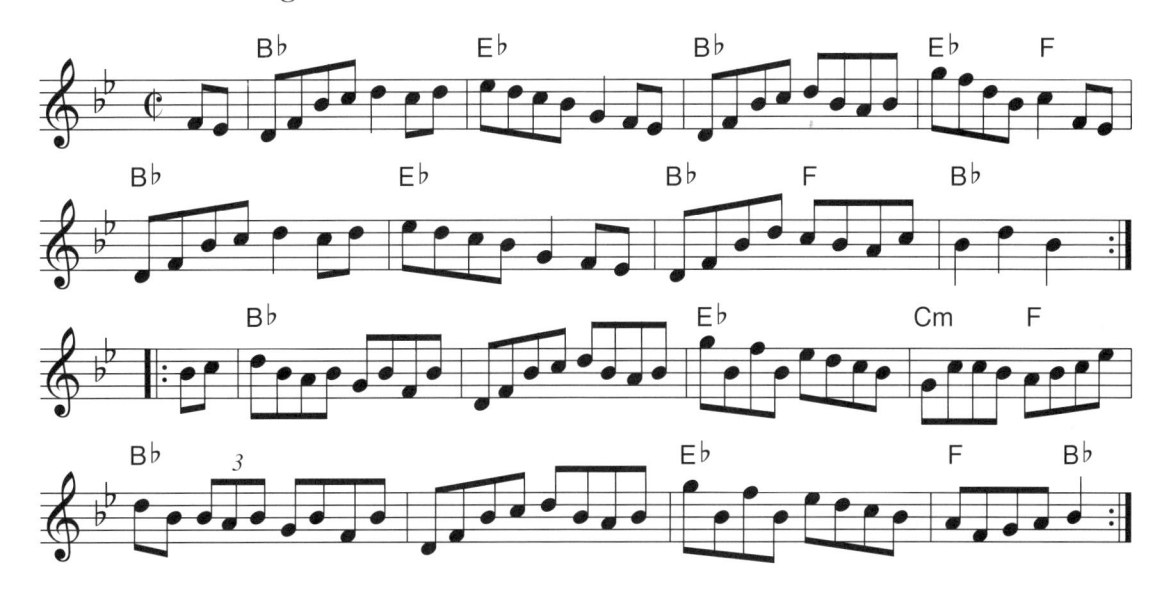

Muckin' o' Geordie's Byre

Munster Buttermilk

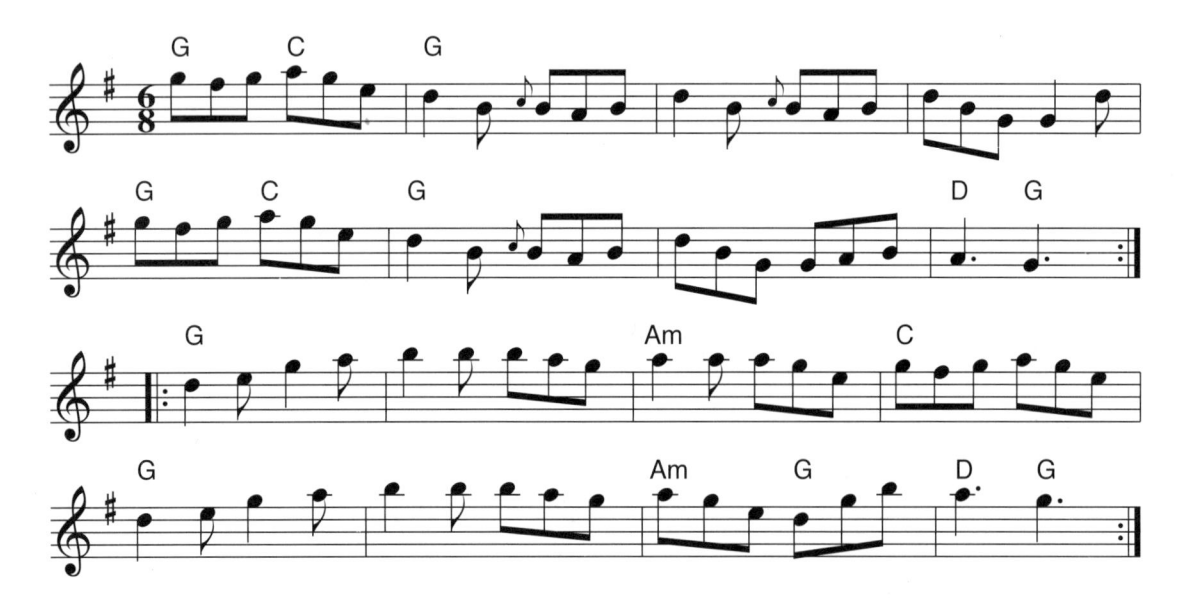

Munster Lass

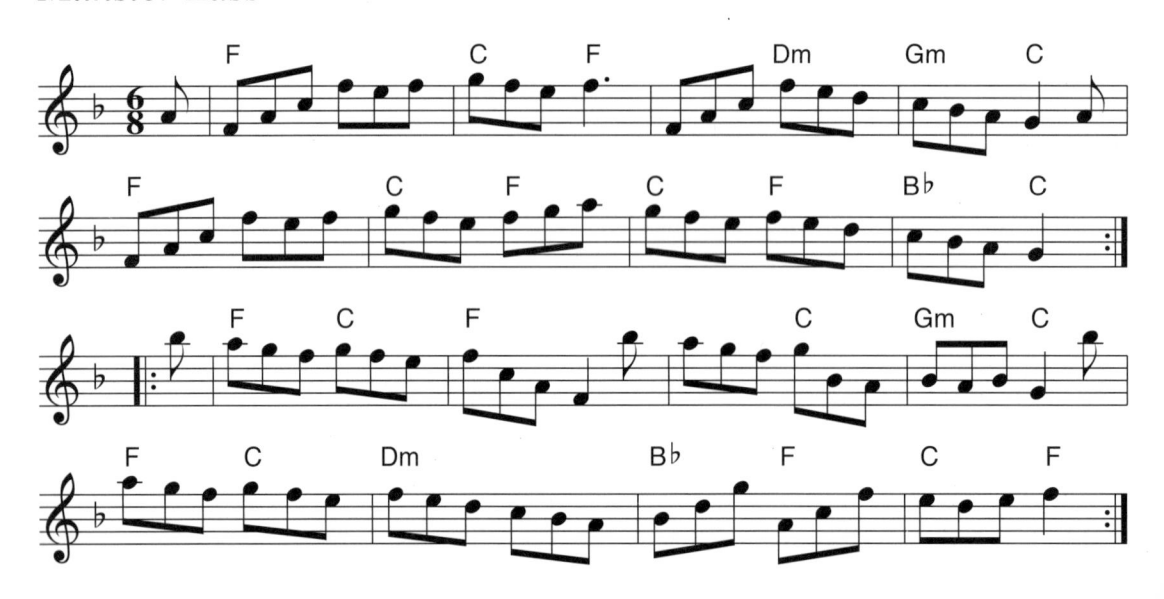

NEW ENGLAND FIDDLER'S REPERTOIRE

My Love's But a Lassie

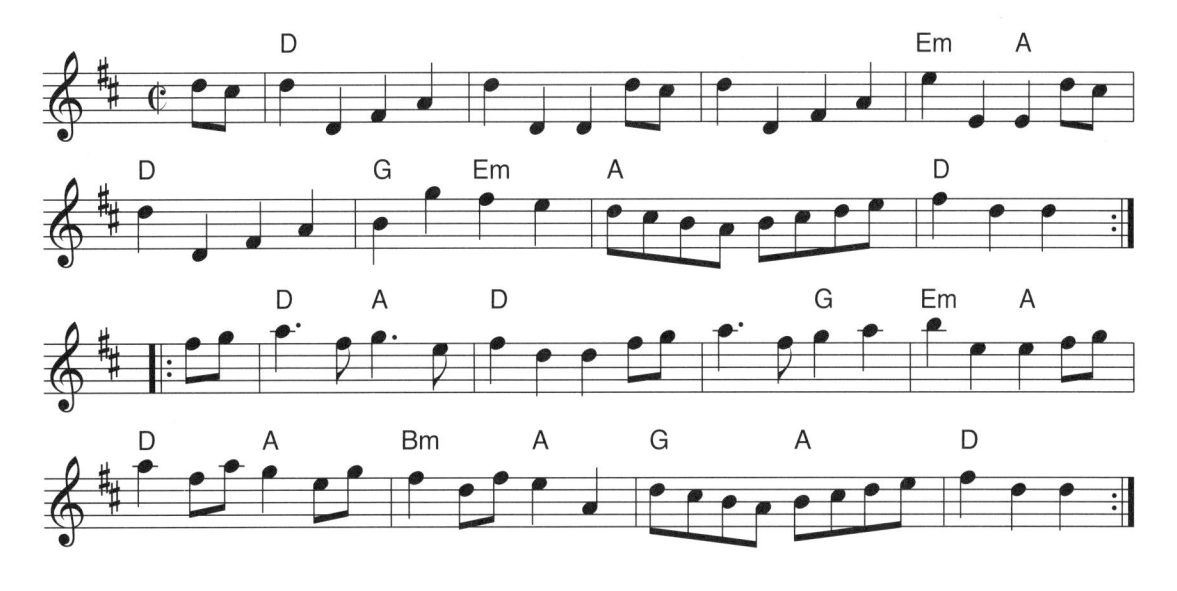

New Rigged Ship

O'Donnell Abu

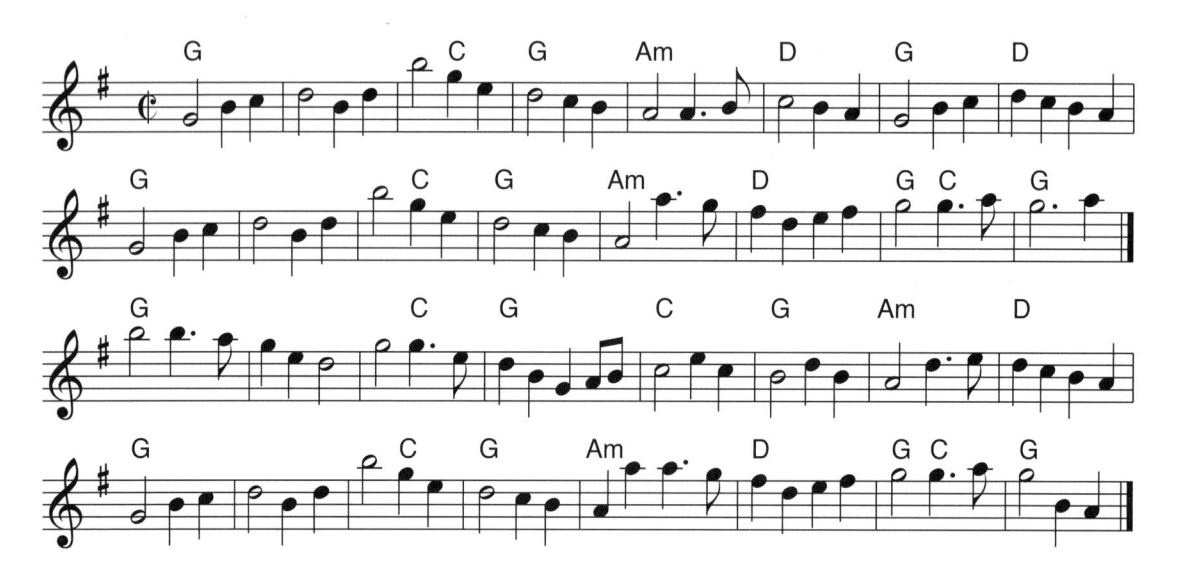

Off She Goes

L'Oiseau Bleu

Old French

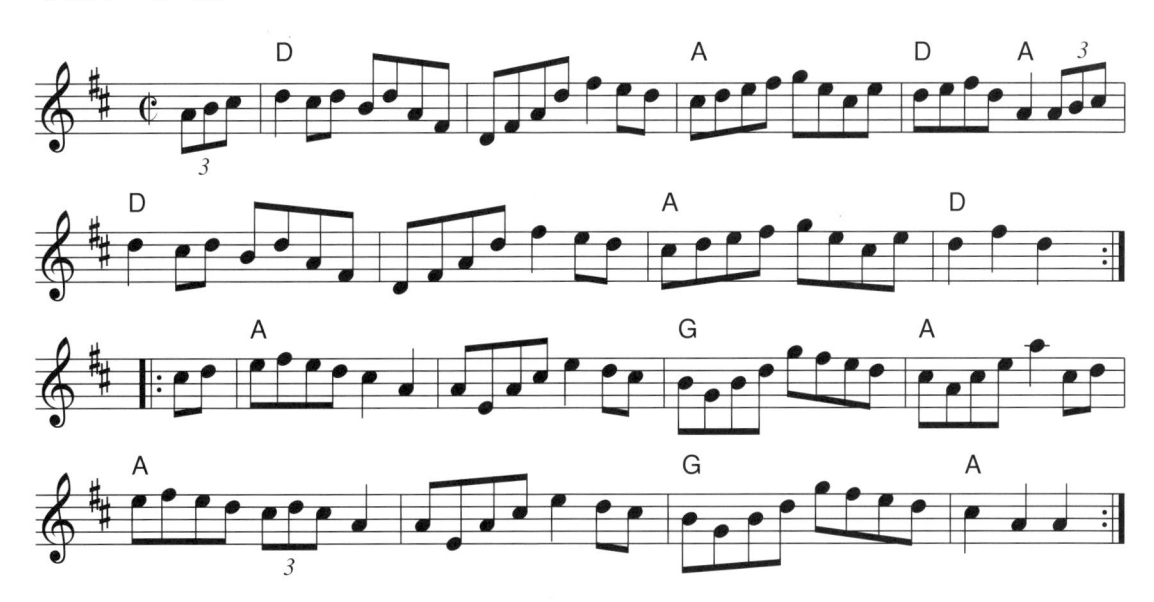

Opera Reel

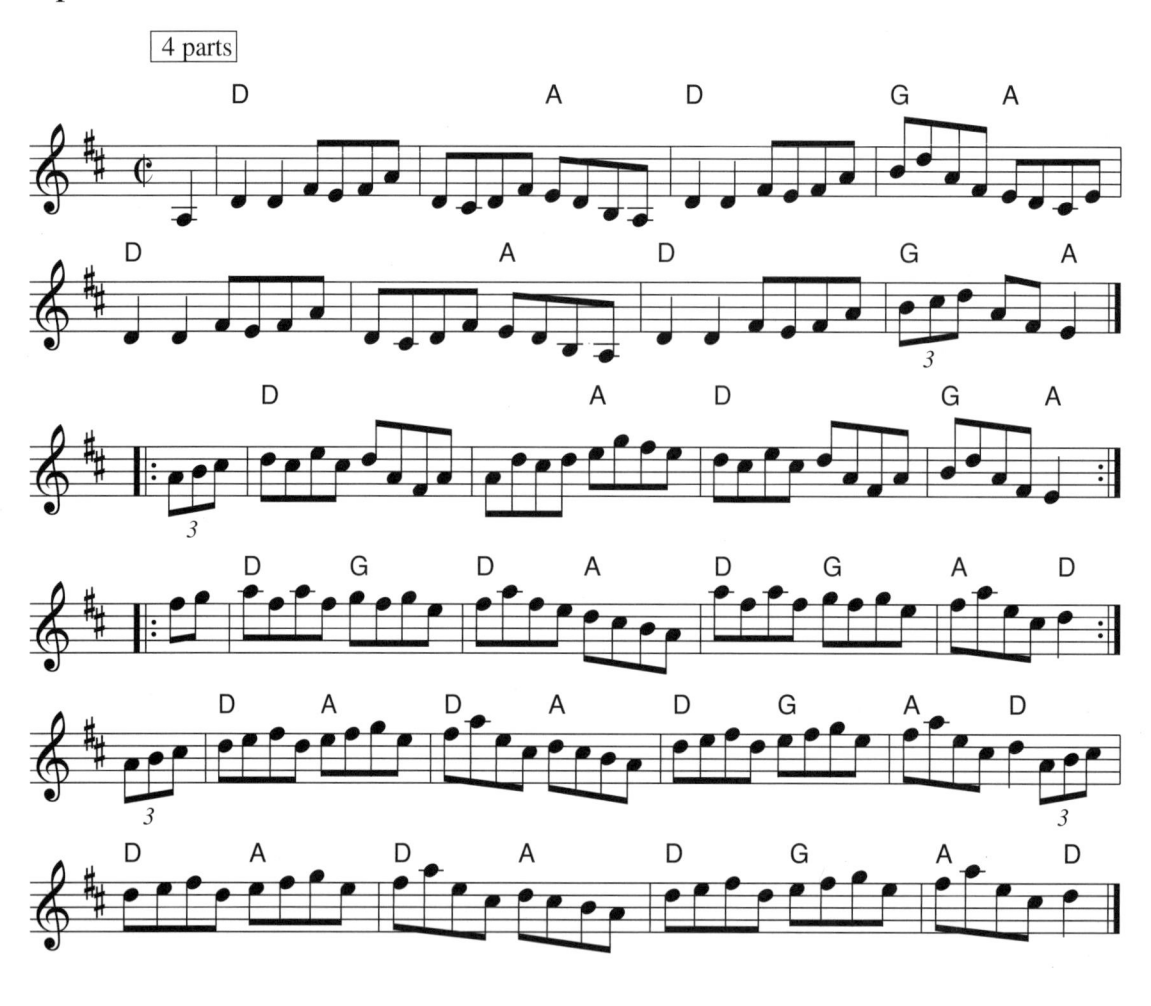

4 parts

Paddy on the Railroad

Paddy on the Turnpike

Paddy Whack

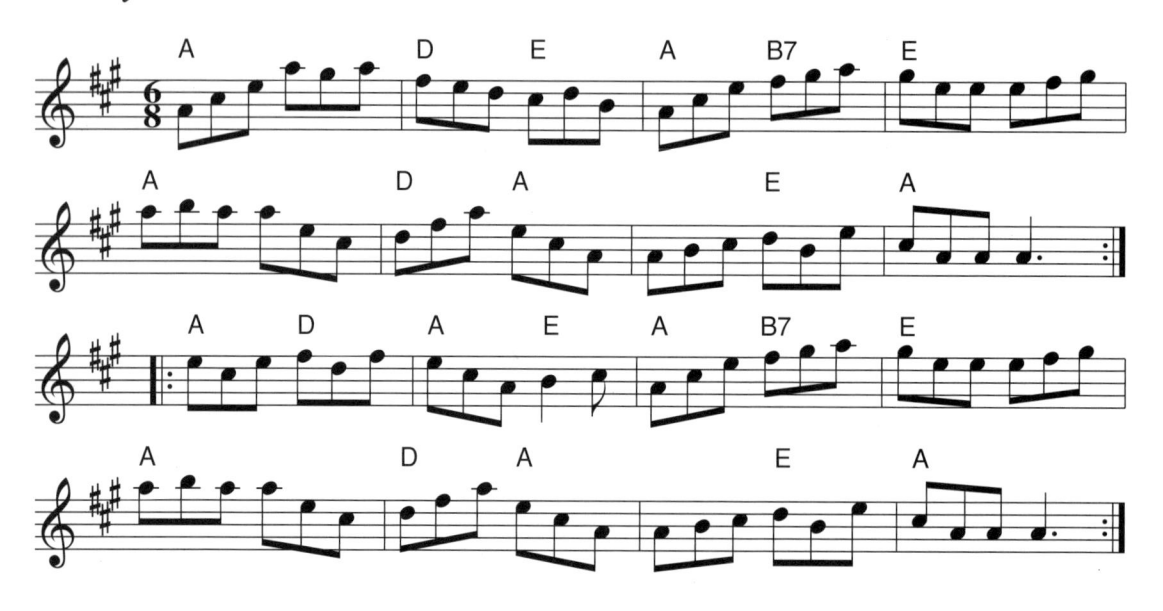

Pays de Haut

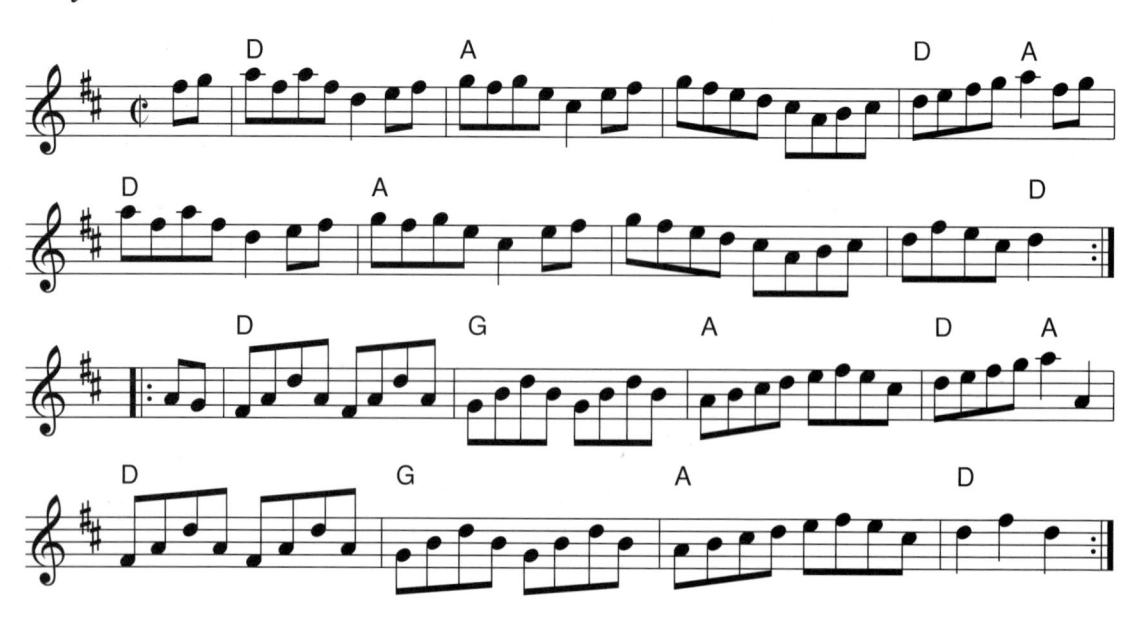

Peter Street

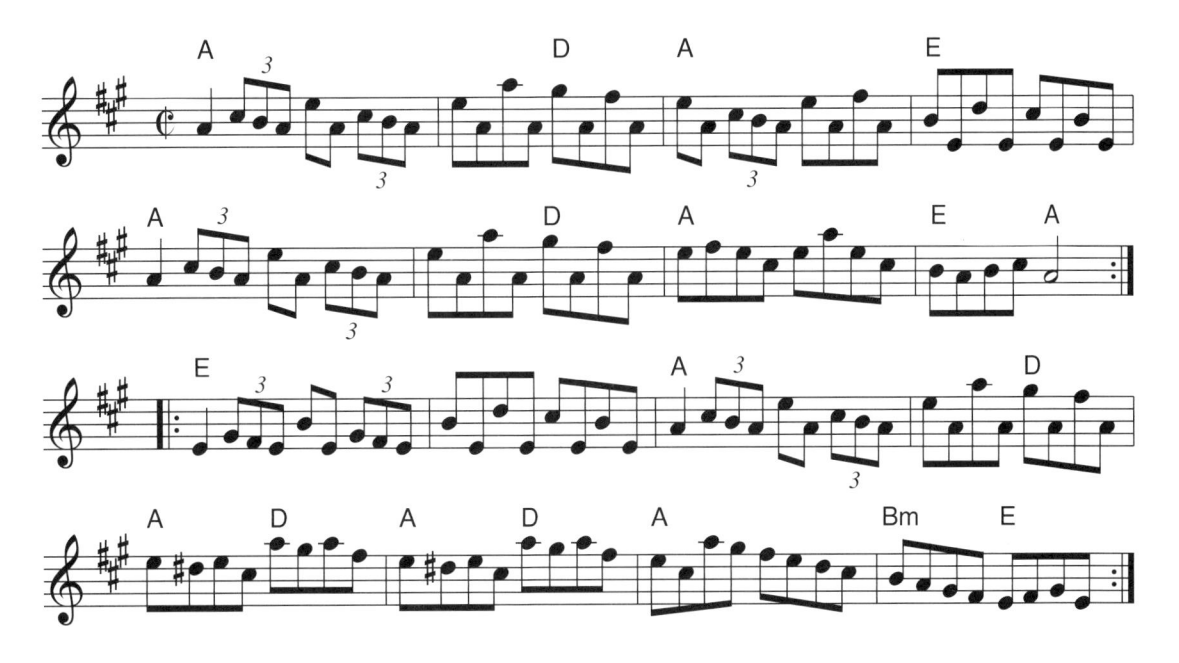

Petronella

Pigtown Fling

Piper's Lass

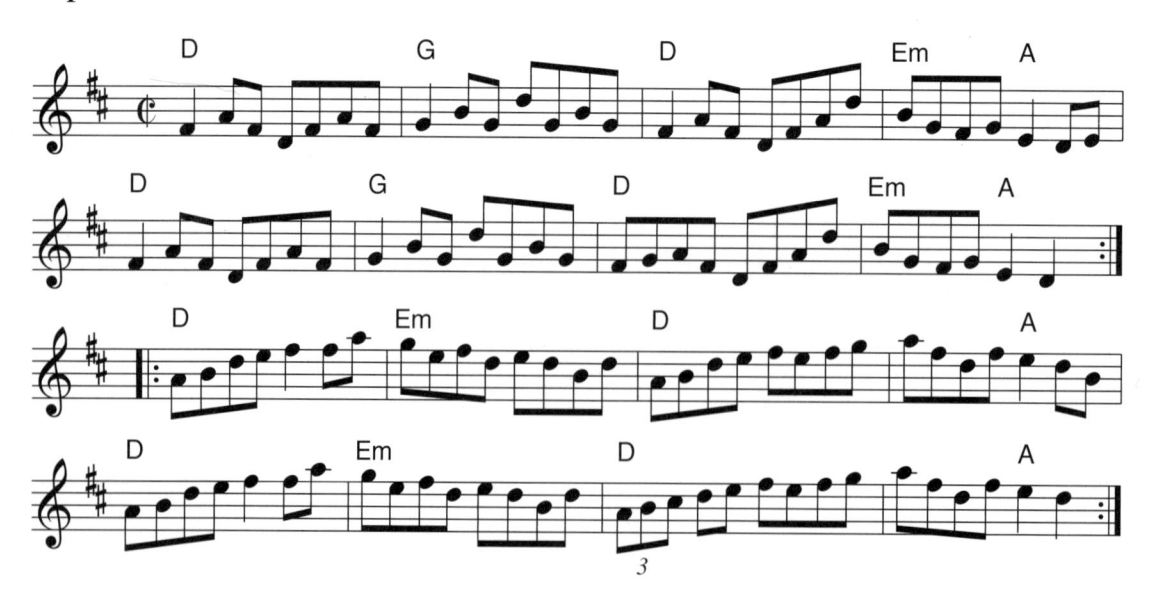

Poppy Leaf Hornpipe

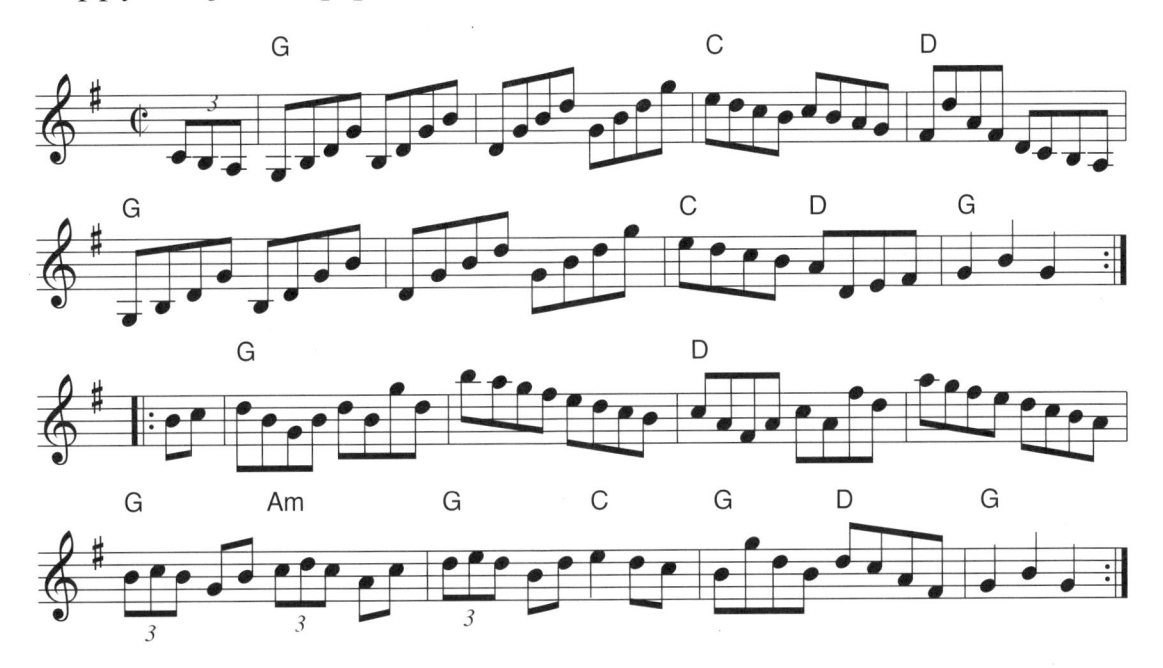

Portland Fancy

4 parts

The reason why the Scotch tunes have liv'd so long, and will probably live forever is merely this, that they are really compositions of melody and harmony united, or rather that their melody is harmony.
–Benjamin Franklin, 1765

President Garfield's Hornpipe

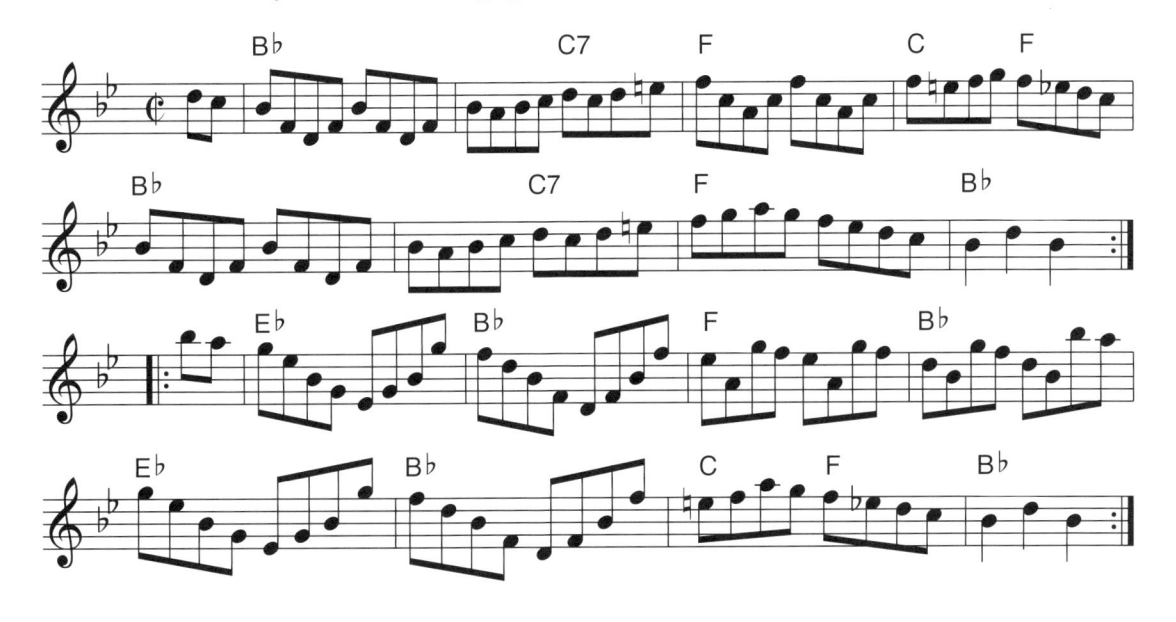

President Grant's Hornpipe

Harry Carleton, c. 1883

President Lincoln's Hornpipe

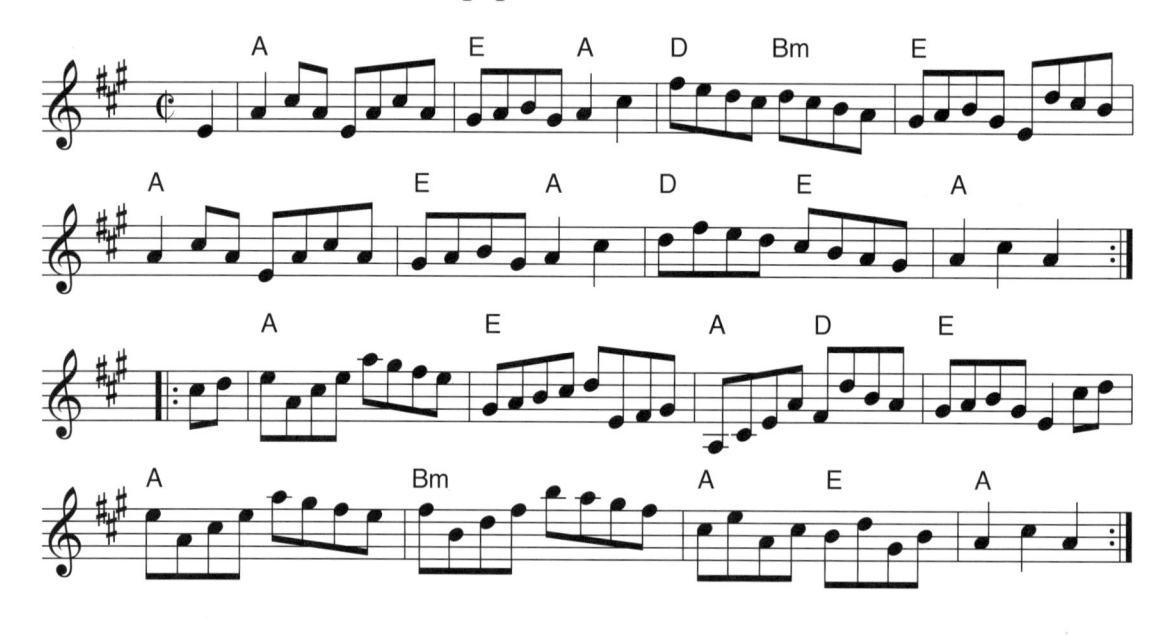

Prince William

Quindaro Hornpipe

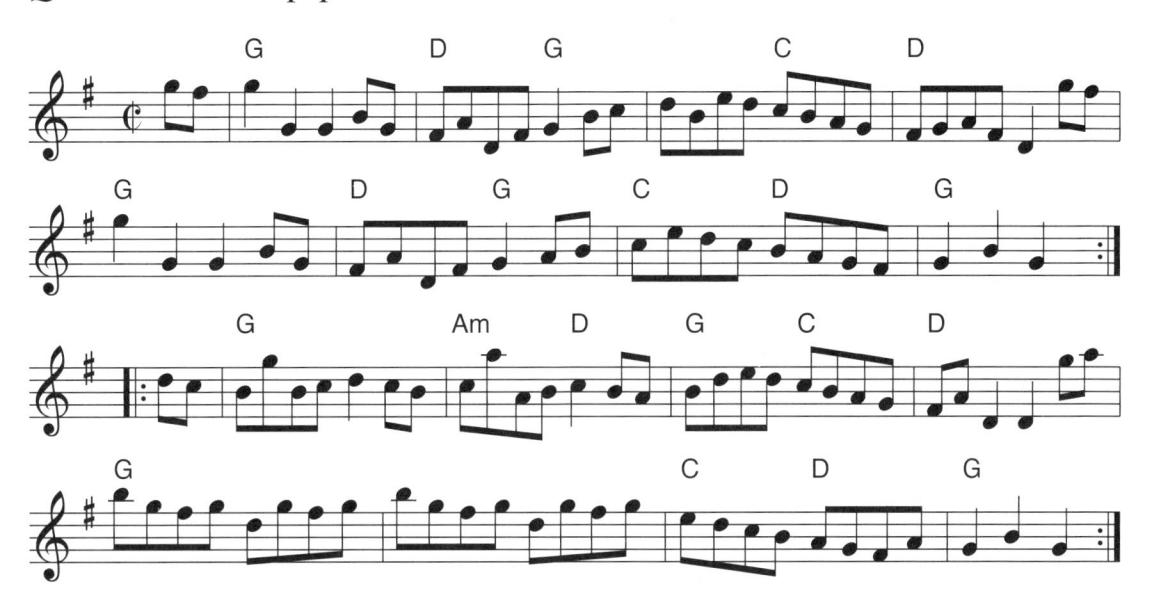

Rakes of Clonmel

March 18. Played for the last contra dance held at the Dublin town hall. The selectmen were closing the upstairs hall after it was deemed a fire hazard. It was packed with 200 dancers.

–Randy Miller, dance diary, 1978

Rakes of Mallow

Red–Haired Boy

NEW ENGLAND FIDDLER'S REPERTOIRE

Red Lion

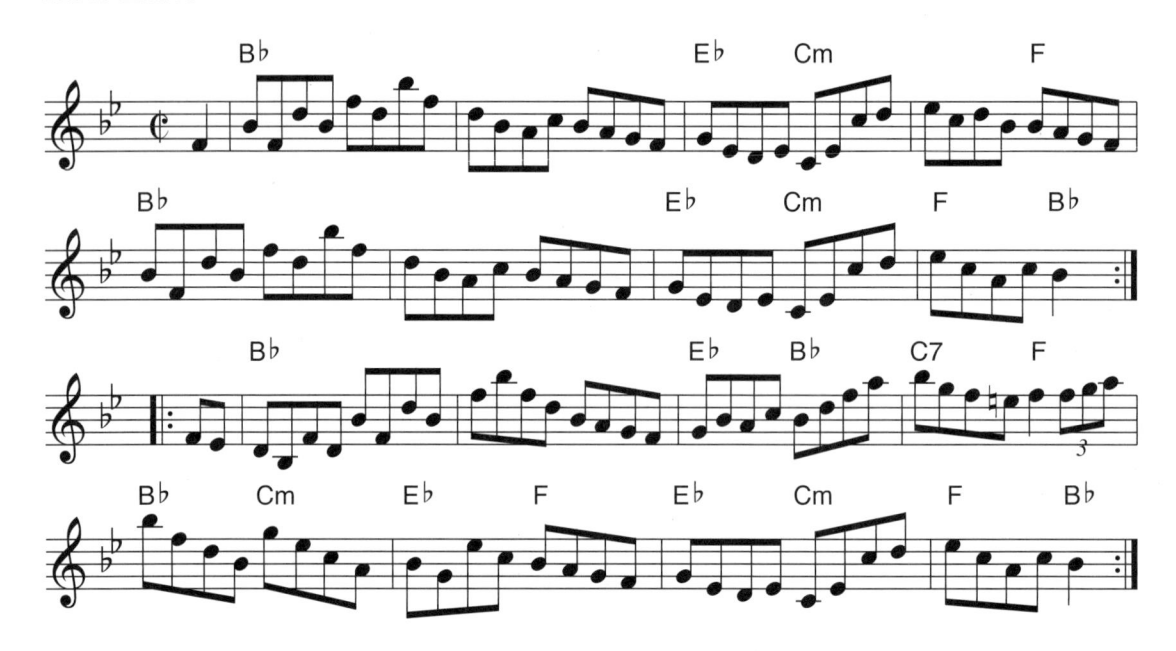

Rickett's Hornpipe

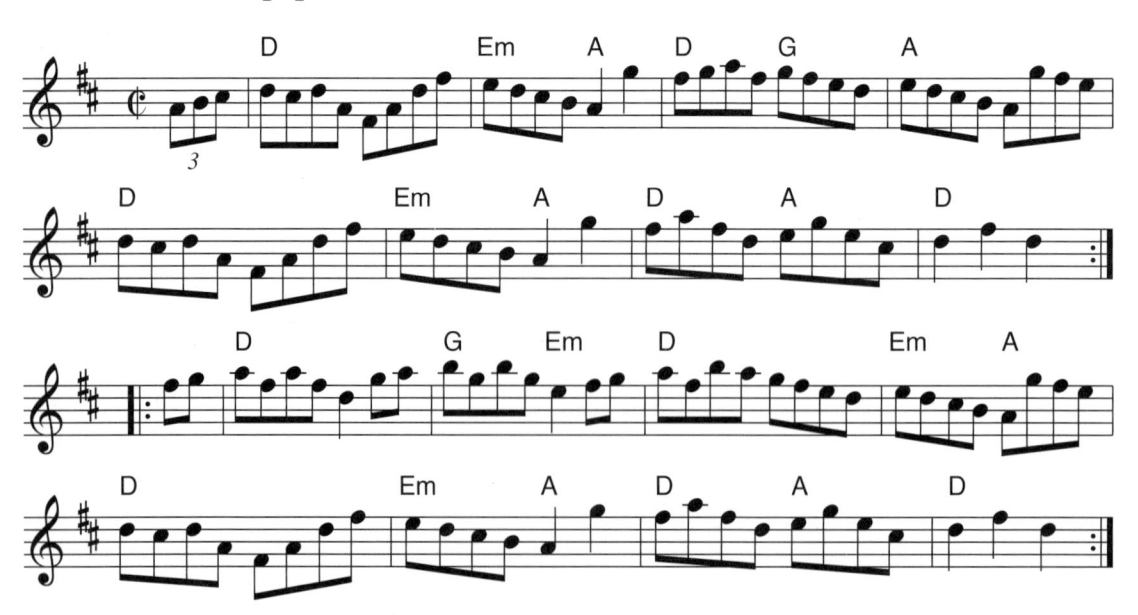

Road to Boston

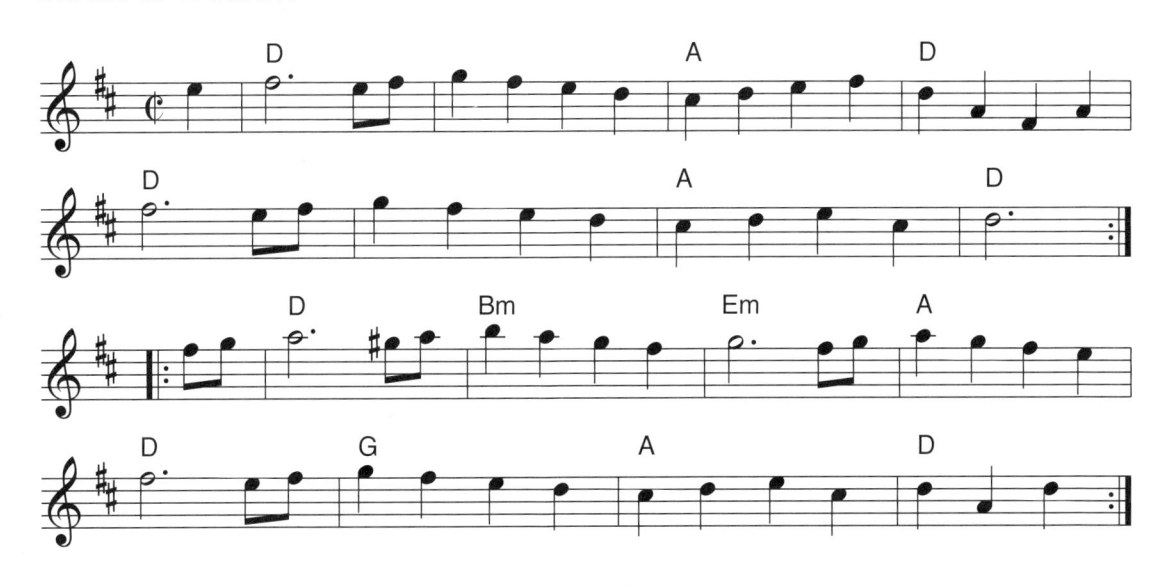

Rock Valley
John Burt

Roddy McCorley

Rolling Off a Log

Ronfleuse Gobeil

Rory O'More

Samuel Lover, c. 1837

Rose Tree

Ross's Reel #4

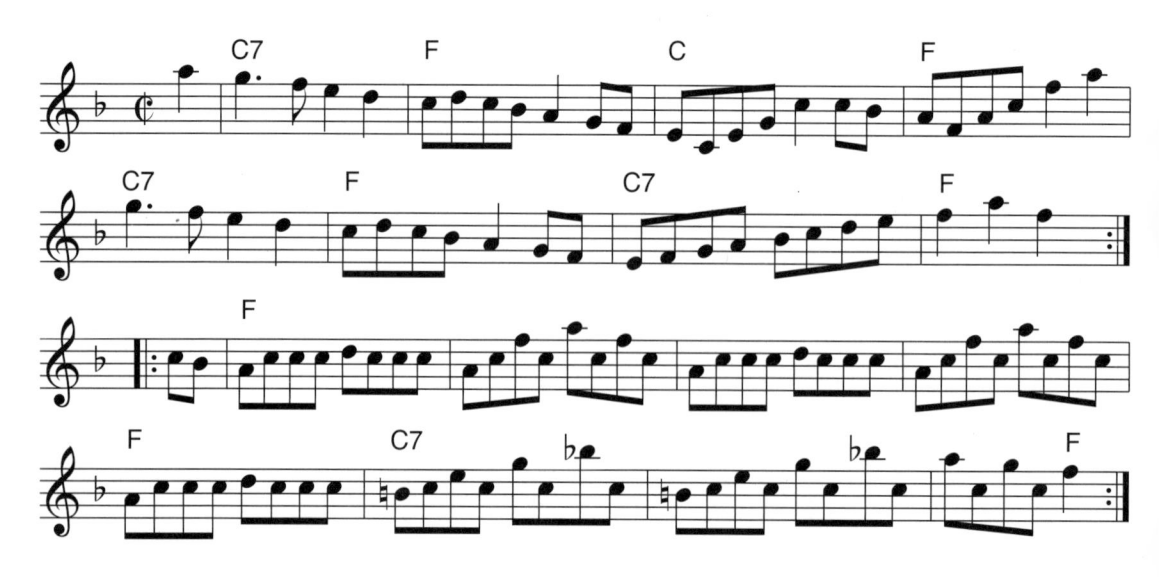

Saddle the Pony

St. Anne's Reel

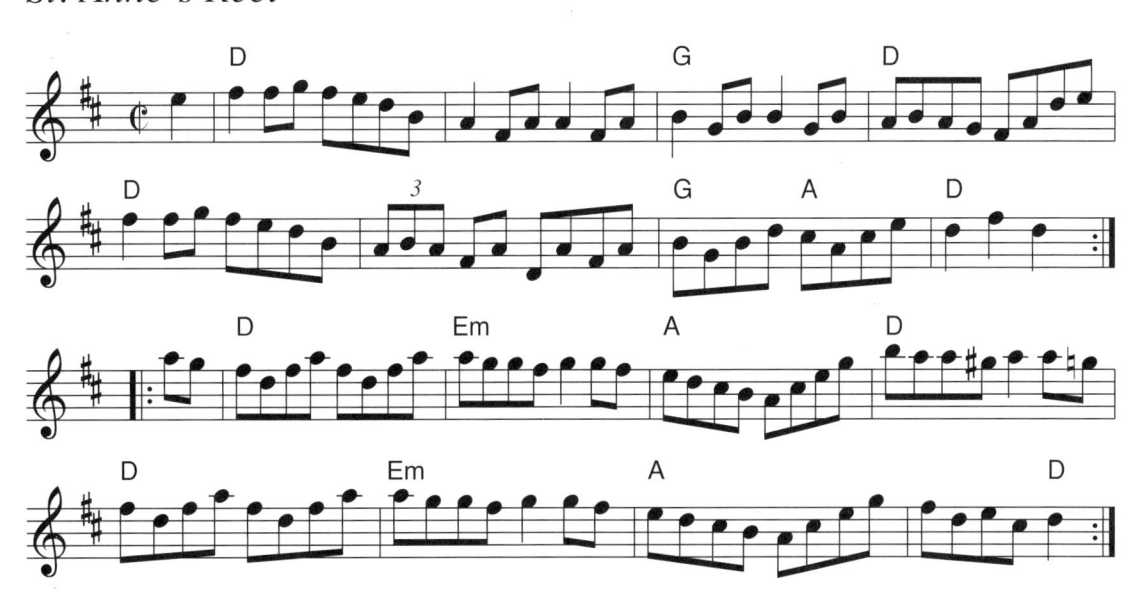

St. Lawrence Jig

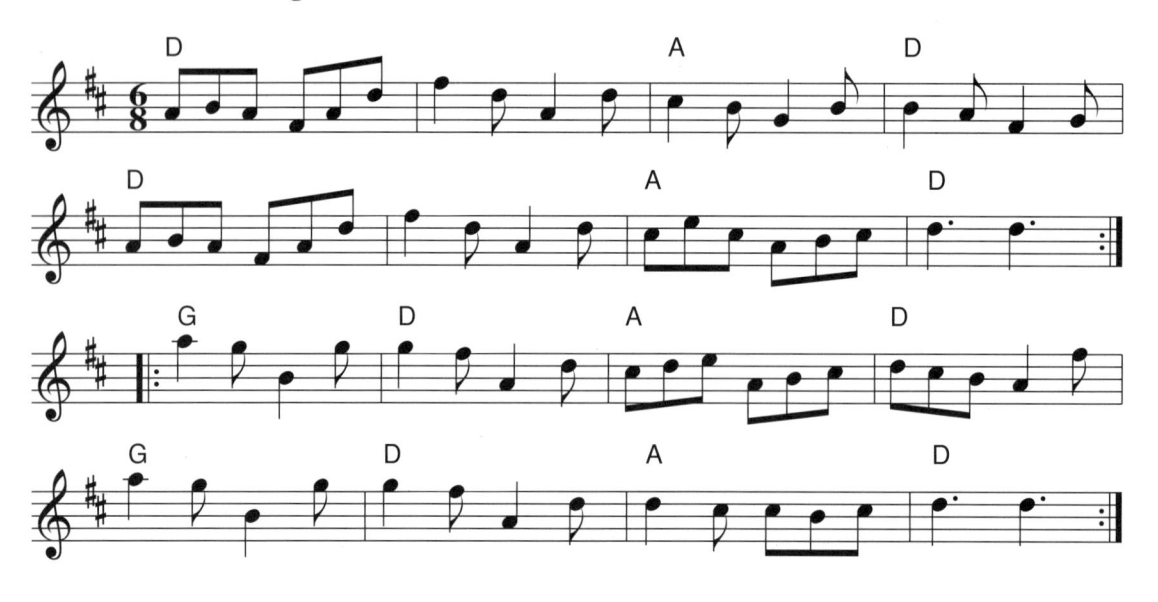

St. Patrick's Day in the Morning

Scotch Hornpipe

Set de la Baie St. Paul

Shandon Bells

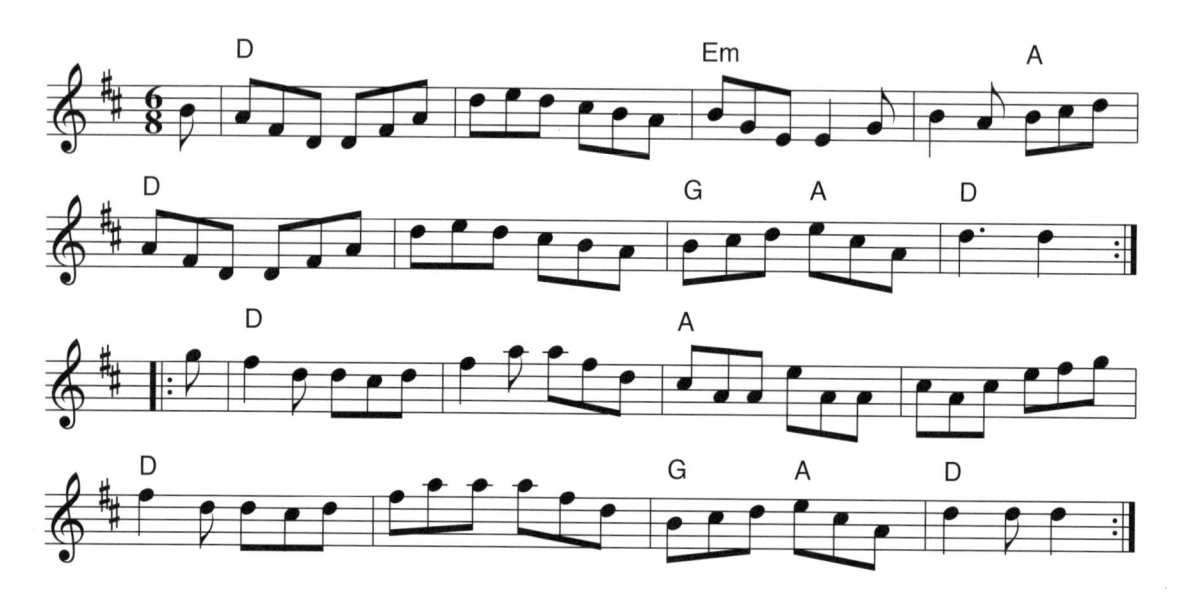

Sheehan's Reel

Ships are Sailing

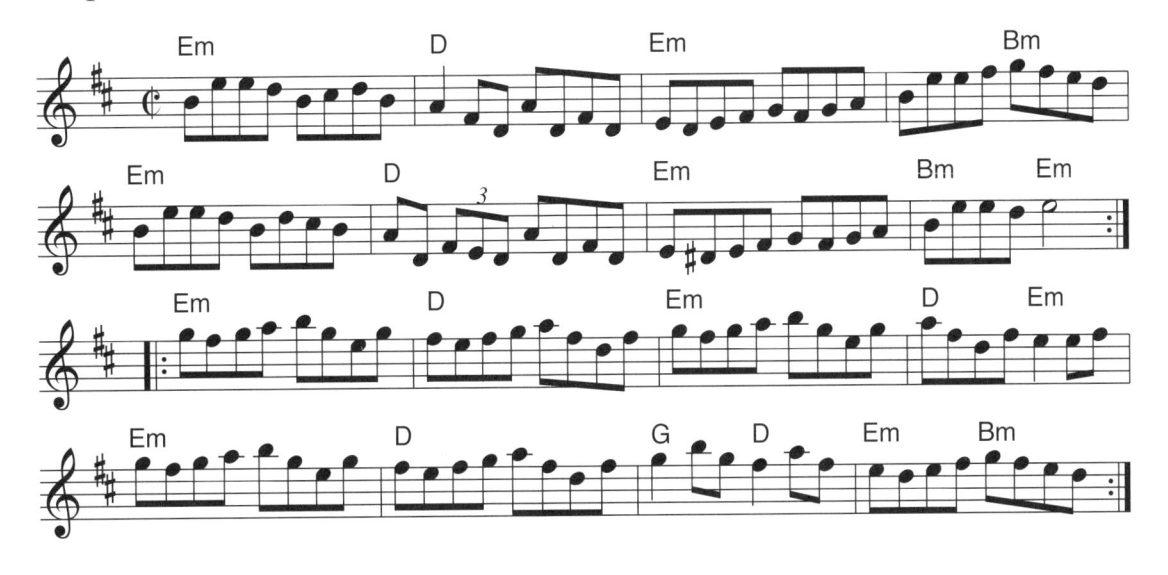

November 16. Played at a riotous dance for a Young Farmers group in Putney, Vermont. Got paid 30 bucks and a box of apples.
—Randy Miller, dance diary, 1978

Smash the Windows

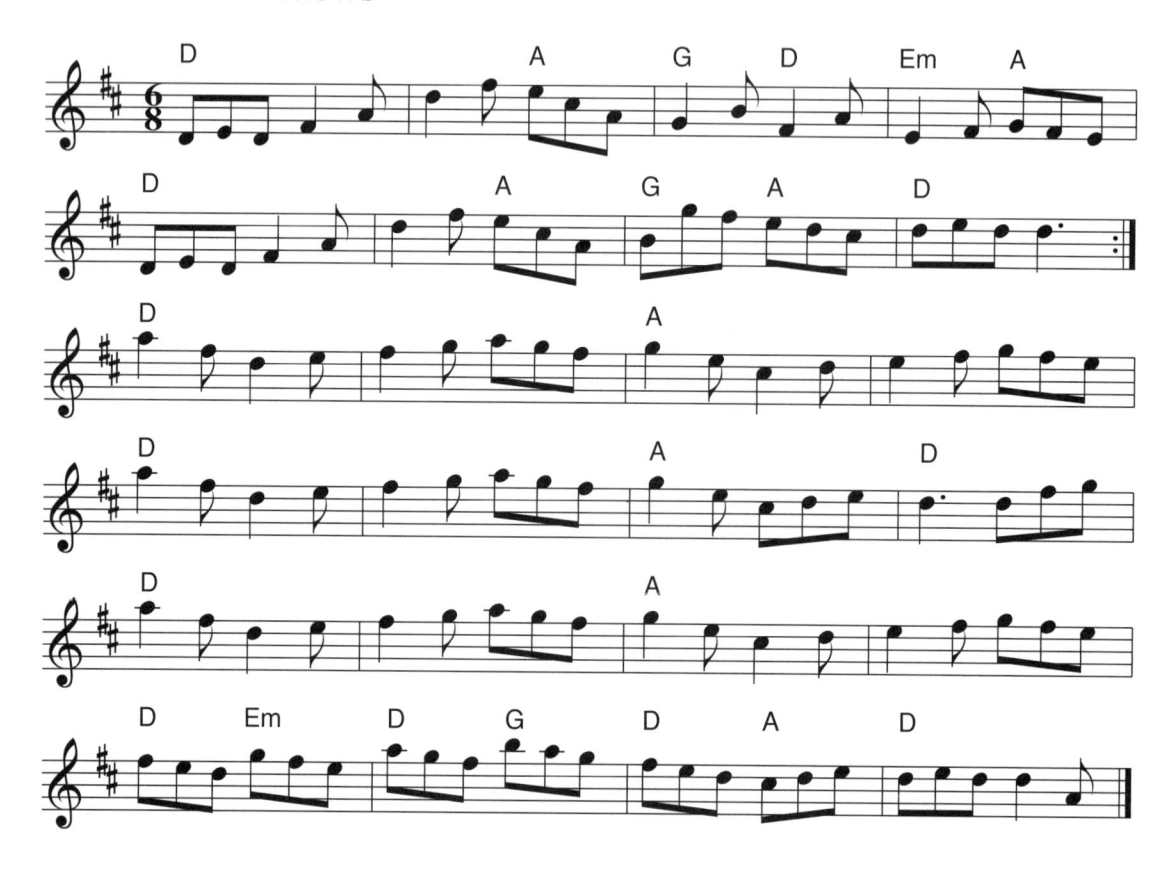

Smith's Reel

Snowflake Hornpipe

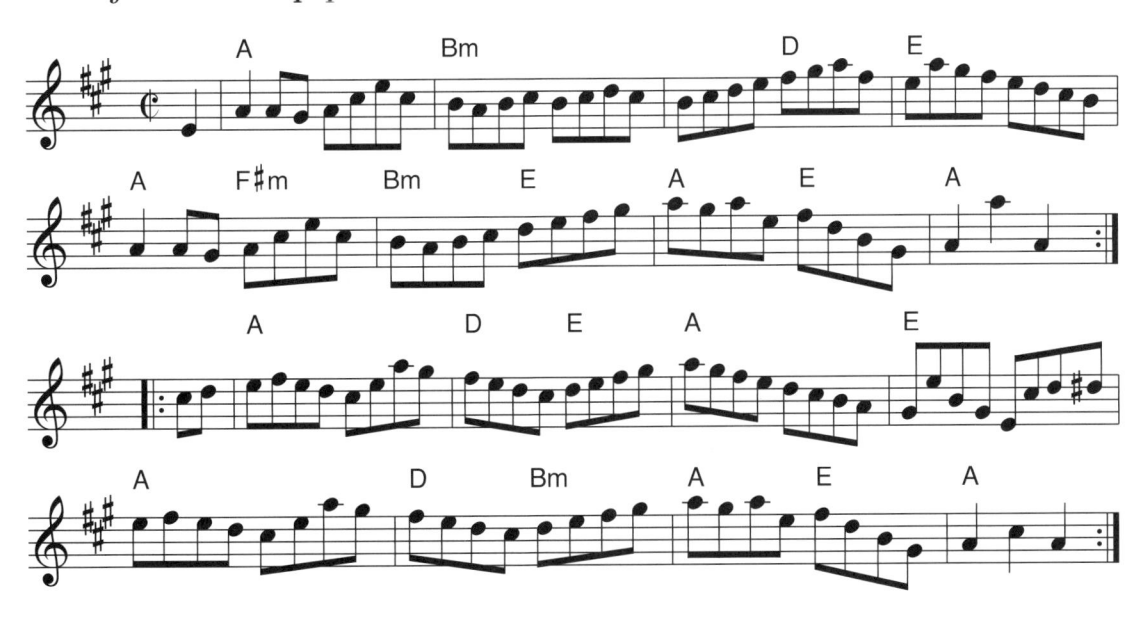

Snowshoer's Reel

Snowy-Breasted Pearl

Soldier's Cloak

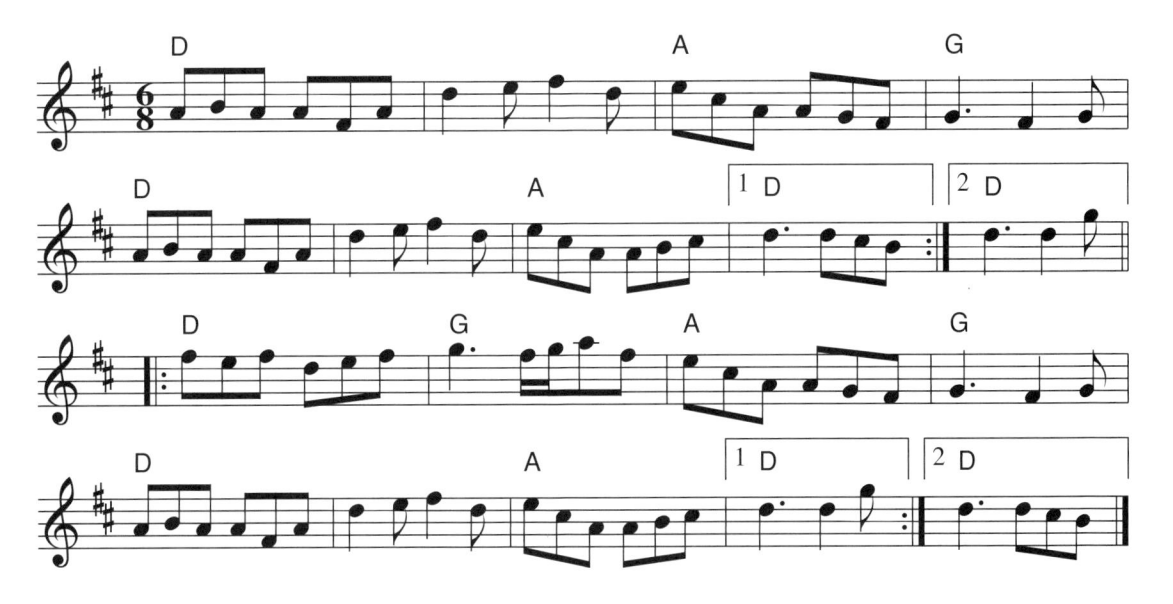

Speed the Plow

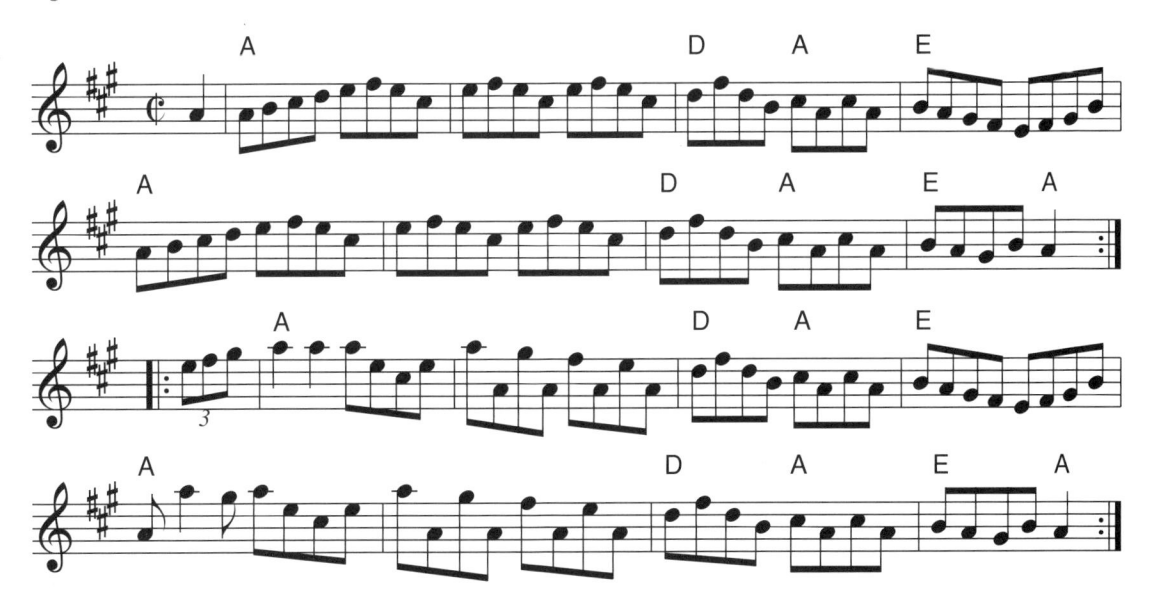

As played by fiddler Albert Quigley, Nelson, N.H. Transcribed from "Traditional and Ethnic New England Square Dance Music, 1955-1957," cassette tape available from Dudley Laufman, Canterbury, N.H.

Spitfire Reel

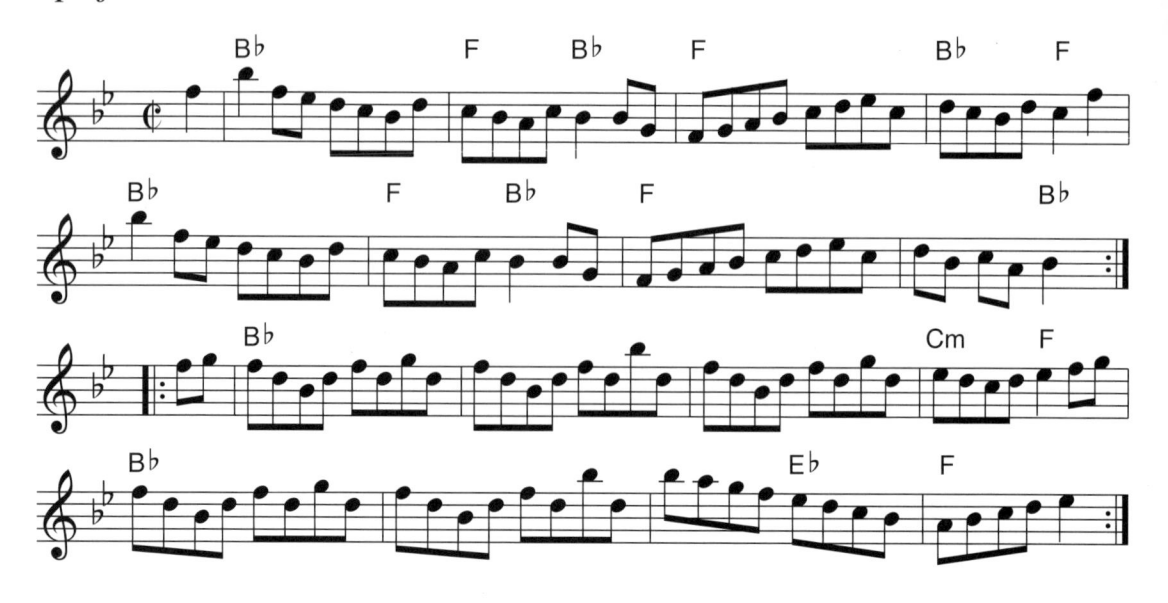

Starr Label Reel

Starry Night for a Ramble

Staten Island Hornpipe

Steamboat Quickstep

Stool of Repentance

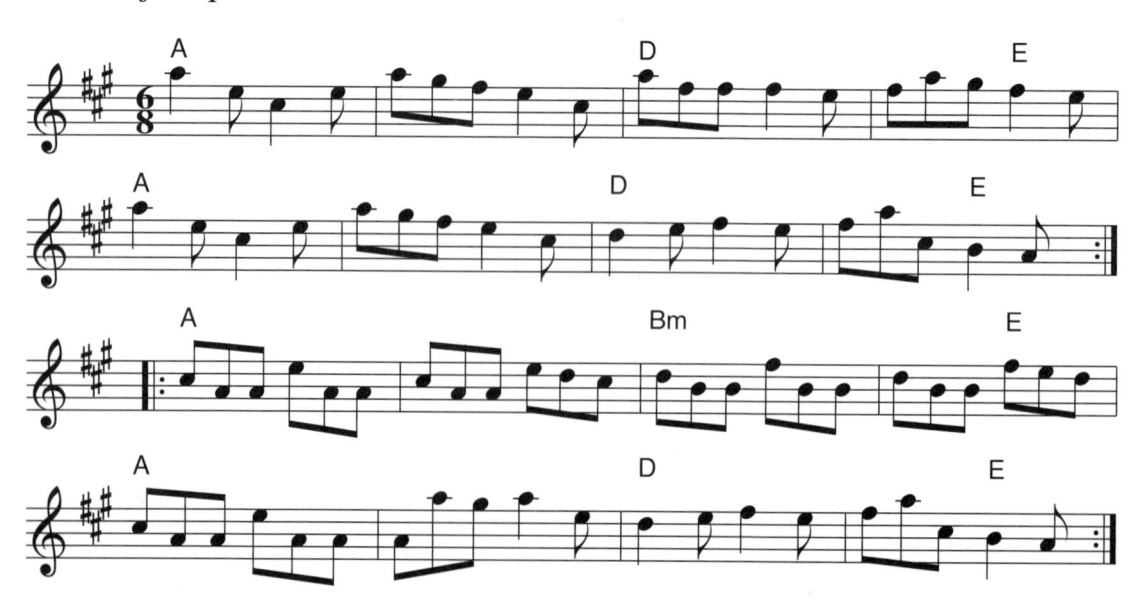

NEW ENGLAND FIDDLER'S REPERTOIRE

Swallowtail Jig

Swallowtail Reel

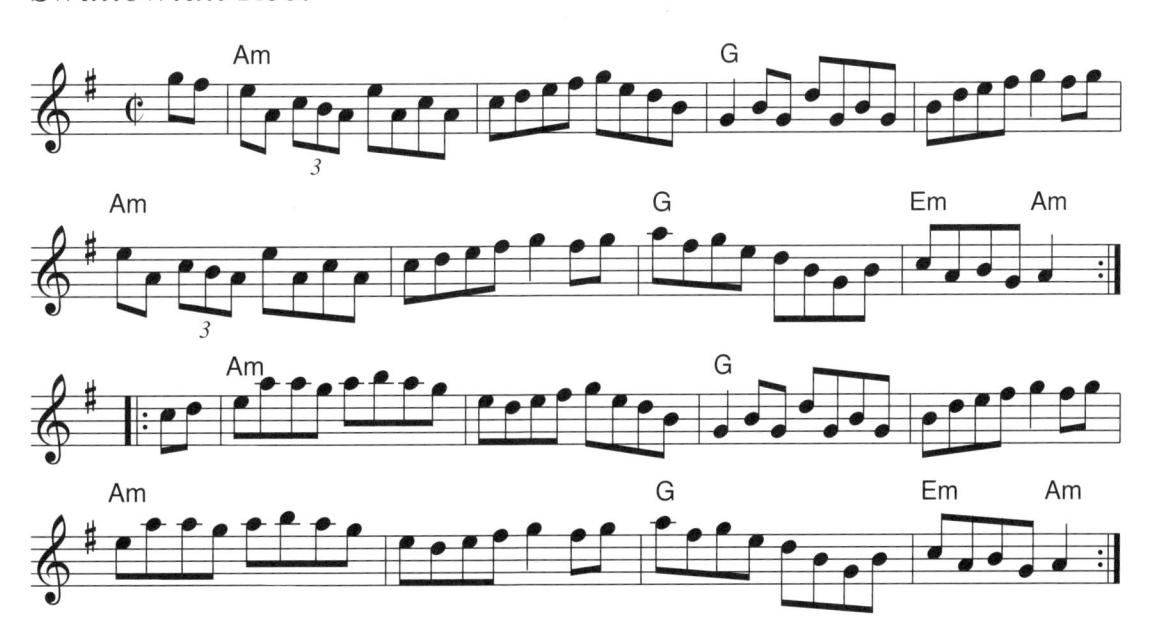

Swinging on a Gate

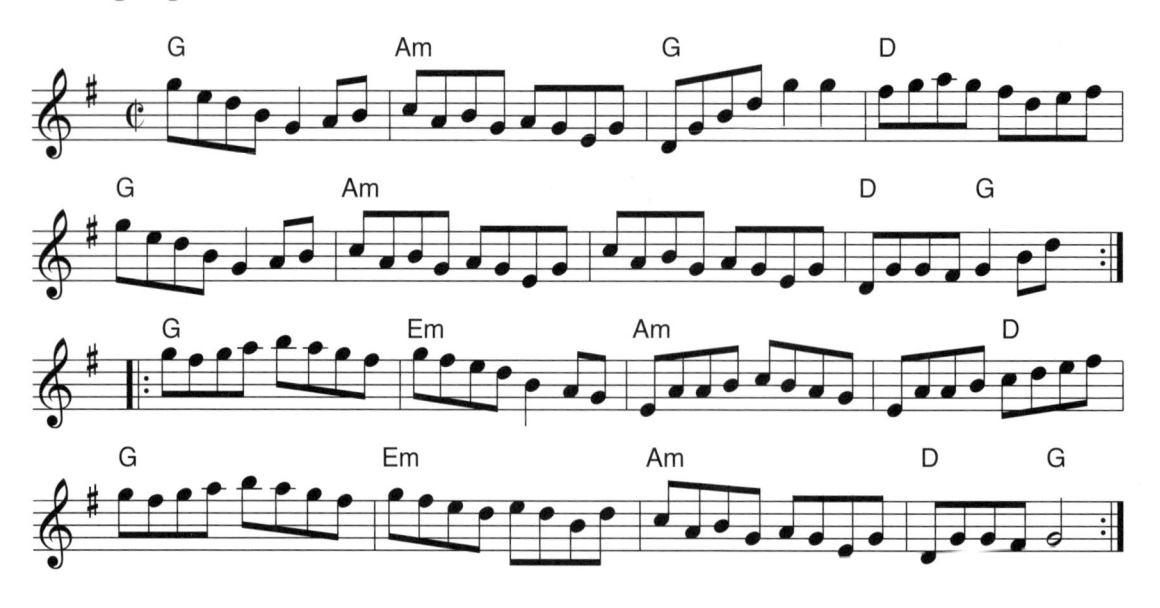

Teetotaler's Reel

The Tempest

He has such a wonderful time playing that his joy is easily projected all through the dance hall. That, of course, is the essence of a real fiddler.
—Beth Tolman and Ralph Page, *The Country Dance Book*, 1937

Tenpenny Bit

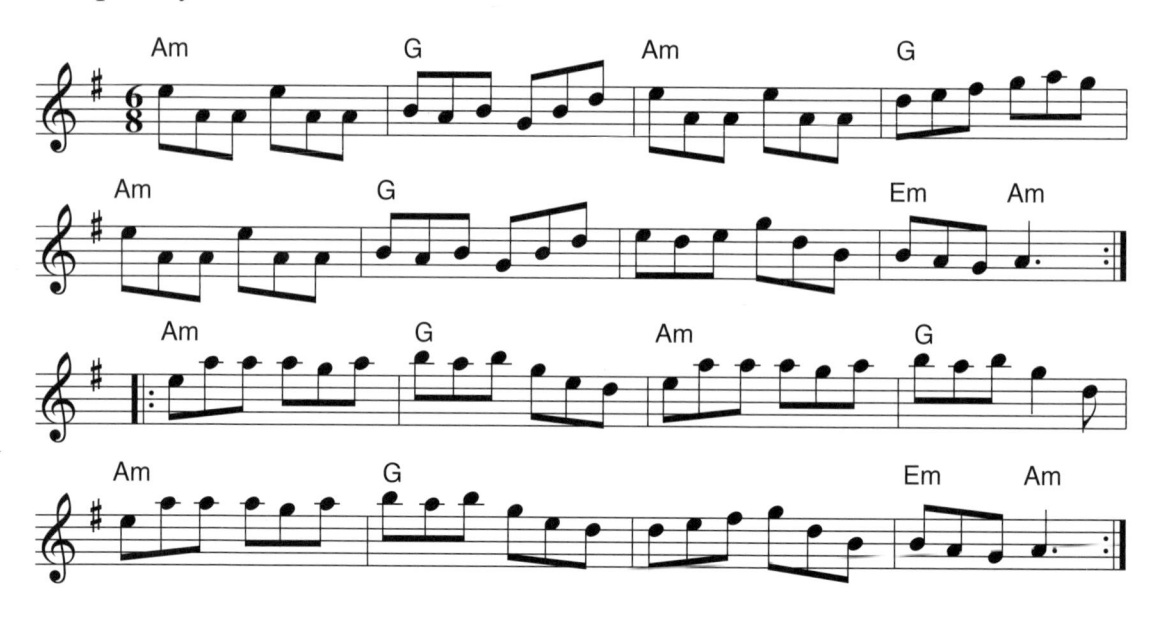

Reel de Ti-Jean

'Tis the Gift to be Simple
Joseph Brackett, 1848

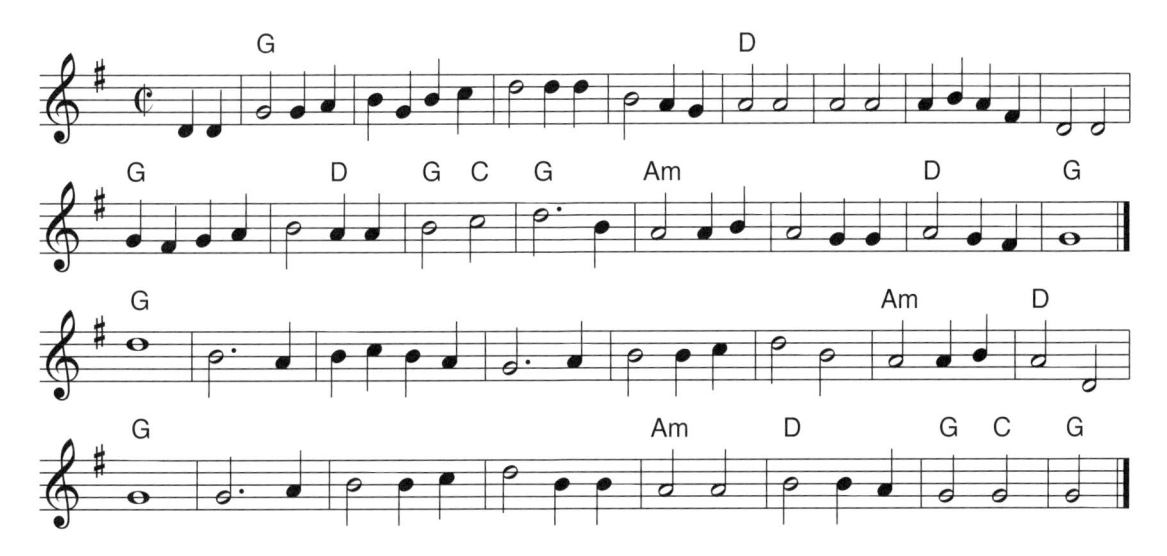

As sung by Sister Mildred Barker, Sabbathday Lake, Maine. "Early Shaker Spirituals," Rounder Records 0078 (1977). Joseph Brackett (1797-1882) was a Shaker elder at Sabbathday Lake.

Top of Cork Road

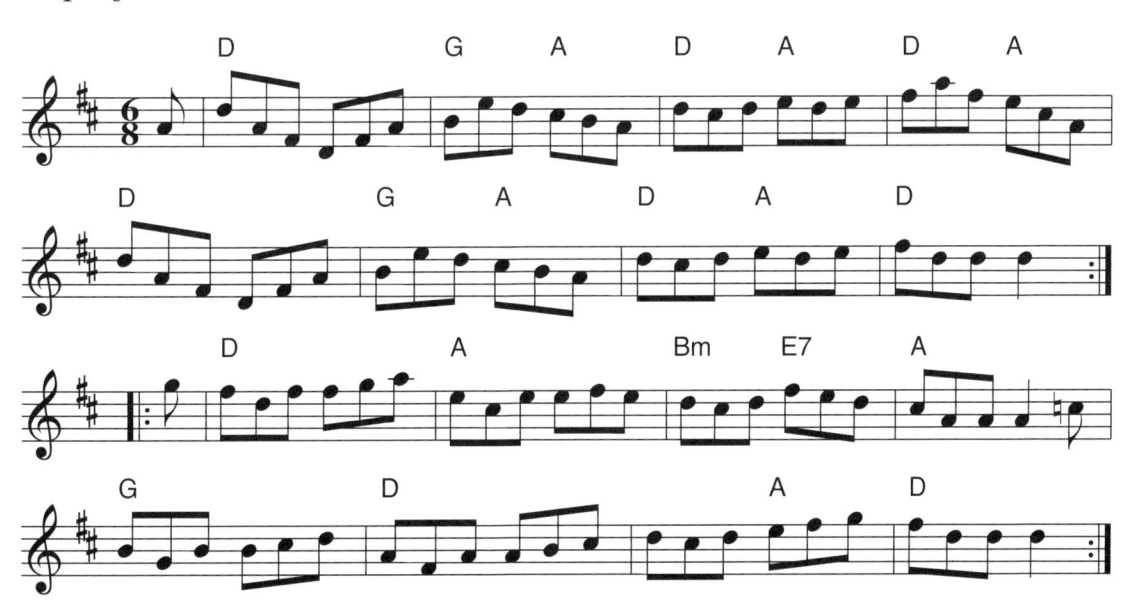

NEW ENGLAND FIDDLER'S REPERTOIRE

La Toque Bleue

Vinton's Hornpipe

Walker Street

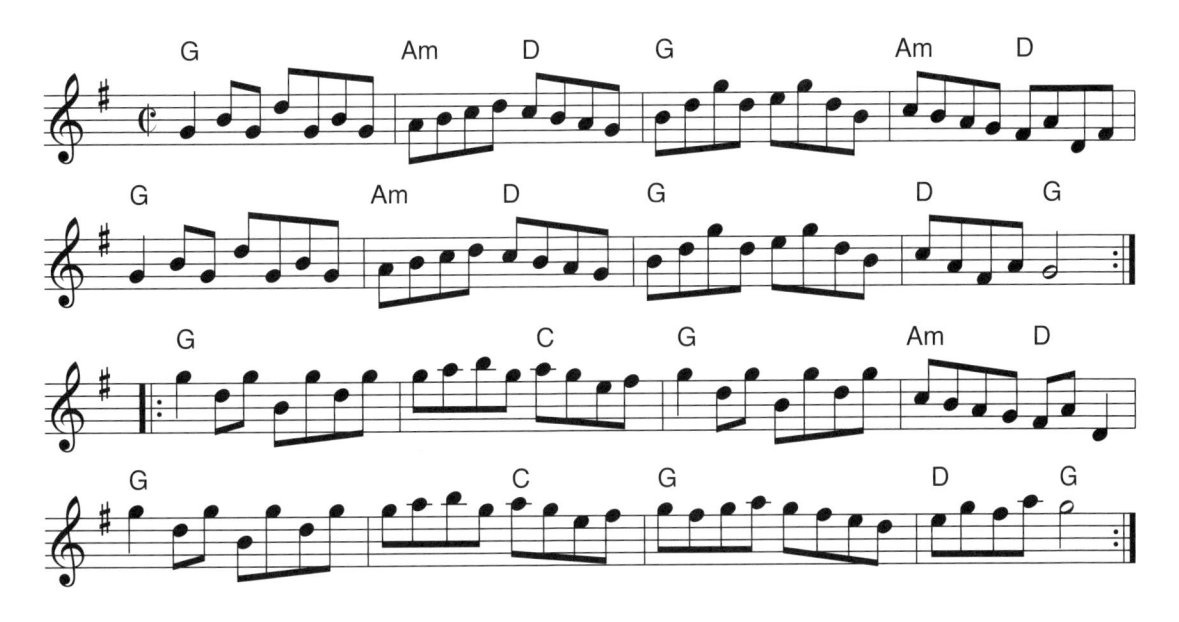

White Cockade

Wind That Shakes the Barley

Woodchopper's Reel

Ned Landry

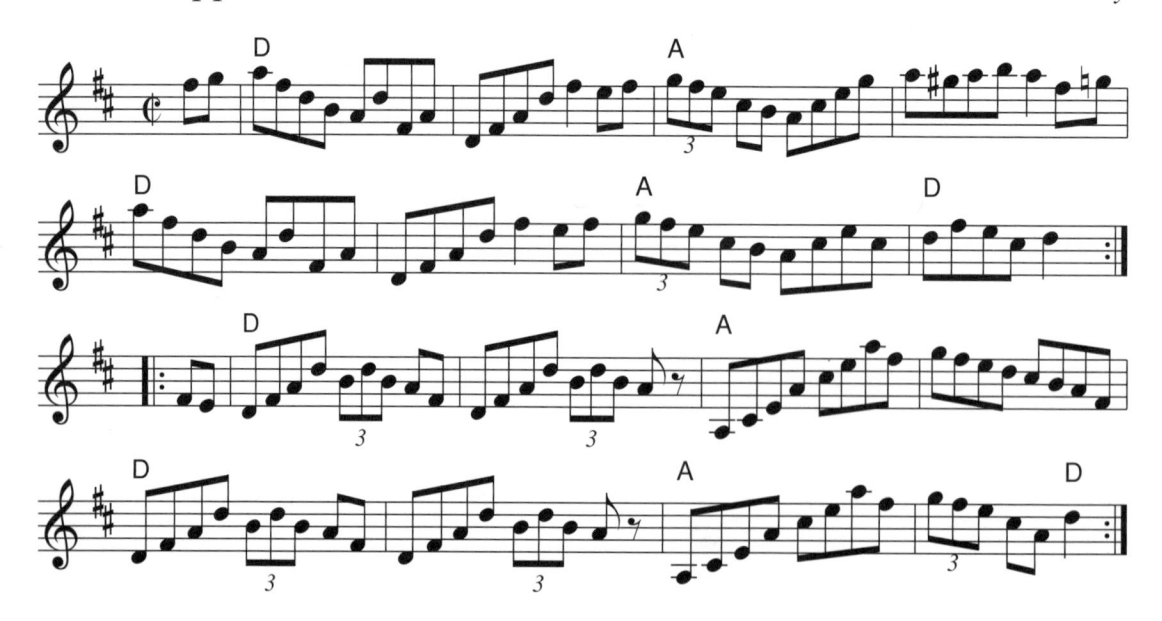

To order Randy Miller's Fiddlecase Books® online, please visit **www.randymillerprints.com**. Each book contains a unique collection of tunes with easy-to-read music, chords, and sturdy coil binding — and it fits in your fiddle case!

New England Fiddler's Repertoire
168 jigs, reels, honrpipes, and marches from the heart of New England: the core repertoire for contra dance musicians. Illustrated with wood engravings by Randy Miller, with an introduction by Newt Tolman. 3rd Edition, 2008.

William Marshall's Scottish Melodies
William Marshall (1748–1833) is regarded as one of the greatest composers of Scottish fiddle music. Born in Fochabers, Scotland, he later became butler to the Duke of Gordon. 262 of Marshall's tunes are included, from his collections published in 1781, 1788, 1800, 1822, 1823, and 1845. This book presents exact replicas of Marshall's tunes, including his dynamics and ornaments, with original bass-clef accompaniments, in a new easy-to-read format. 322 pages, 2nd Edition, 2007.

Irish Traditional Fiddle Music
235 jigs, reels, hornpipes, slip jigs, airs, etc., including 18 polkas new to this edition. Faithful settings of traditional tunes based on the recordings of Michael Coleman, Máirtín Byrnes, Andy McGann, Seán Ryan, Paddy Canny, Julia Clifford, Paddy Cronin, Antóin Mac Gabhann, and others. With chords and extensive notes on sources and tunes. Illustrated. 2nd Edition, 2006.

"Frankly, it's the best Irish tune collection issued for many a long year." –Geoff Wallis, *Musical Traditions*

The Fiddler's Friend
Forty fiddle exercises to improve fingering and bowing by Randy Miller. Randy has used his teaching experience and thirty-five years of fiddling to create a series of exercises tailored to fiddlers and traditional fiddle music. Add nimbleness and fluidity to your playing! For all levels, novice through advanced. 28 pages, illustrated. 2007.

The Fiddler's Throne
375 traditional tunes, including compositions by Liz Carroll, Angus Fitchet, Jerry Holland, Josephine Keegan, Ralph Page, Ed Reavey, Billy McComiskey, and others. A unique, comprehensive collection of old and new tunes from New England, Ireland, Scotland, Cape Breton, and the Shetlands. With chords and notes on the tunes. 2004.

"Highly recommended. A valuable resource for dance musicians." –Mark Sustic, Vermont

The Fiddler's Throne CD
Randy Miller performs three dozen tunes from the *Fiddler's Throne* book on fiddle and solo piano. Accompaniment by guitarists Tom Hodgson and David Loney, with Will Miller, bodhrán. Sample sound files online. 2005.

"These tracks are a real treat in the way they combine the old and the new. Miller's music is the real deal." –Mary DesRosiers, *Sing Out!* Winter 2006